CW00919287

To Ally,

Who has walked with me through it all.

Forgive me, and tell me again that it was worth it?

Andrew.

To Jordan and to Joel,

Who have seen my successes and my failures.

Don't be scared to make mistakes, embrace adventure.

Dad.

A manual for living by faith

Foreword

So, you want to be a missionary?

Modern day missionaries. We had a tough job with how to describe ourselves. Those "sending" us had a terminology where missionary fitted, but I was an Accountant, my wife a Teacher. Some who were supporting us in this venture were not Christian, but believed in us and/or believed in the good we were going to do. They were interested in the outcomes and couldn't care much about the Gospel, if at all. To them, the Gospel got in the way and we were voluntary workers, or charity workers. To those we were going out to, how would they react to us being "missionaries"? What would that say to them about how we saw them, how we valued them? This, our job description, was and continues to be, quite a complex question.

What was clear however, seeing as we were not of independent means, and didn't have pots of money sitting around, was that we would needed to find a way of financially underpinning this endeavour. We needed money to eat, for somewhere to live, for travel, for vaccinations. Travelling with young children meant we needed to send them to school and provide some kind of stability.

We therefore needed to fund raise. Many of the books available weren't particularly suited to our circumstance or our British culture. We blundered about, lurching from one potential disaster to another.

However, in over seven years of full time voluntary/missionary activity, we survived and even thrived. We loved that season. It was not always easy, but it was good.

This book brings together the lessons of our successes, and the lessons from our failures. Do yourself a favour and learn what you can before you start. The rest you'll probably have to blunder about with like we did.

There are three sets of potential missionaries that might need this book. And a fourth.

1. You're independently wealthy, so do not need to raise additional funds. But, you will find it so much better in the long run if you can take a group of people along for the ride with you.
2. You're going to join an established mission organisation who will likely help with some, or most, but not all of your funding.
3. You're young (or old) and haven't got anywhere near enough money coming in that will support you. You're desperately seeking help!
4. Your mum!

It will stretch your faith and bring you closer to God than ever before. We are most grateful for that, you will likely be too, one day, when you look back!

"The two most important days of your life are the day you were born, and the day you find out why." Mark Twain

Luke 22:27b Jesus said "I am among you as one who serves."

A manual for living by faith

Introduction

Living a (more) full life

We spent two years in the Caribbean serving a Bible College and a number of small faith based local charities, then later, four years or so with YWAM in the US, Asia and Europe. During those days, as a family, we had to rely upon God in a way that I've found it tough to do back in the world that most of us inhabit.

When you don't have enough money, but are living and working your calling, in some far flung place bereft of your normal support networks and structures, calling out and desperately seeking God, hoping and expecting God to deliver, becomes very easy indeed!

I sit at a desk at Quarr Abbey on the Isle of Wight, taking a few days out from the hustle and bustle and hassle and strain of my job as a Finance Director. Seeing the Benedictine Monks living out their lives, utterly dedicated to their calling, reminds me of a time when I once did that too.

I miss it. I miss relying upon God, I miss accidentally seeking out ever more creative ways for God to show up. I tend to reach for a tablet when I get a headache, use an overdraft when I have more month left than money, or book trips away on a credit card, paying for it sometime in the months following. It's too easy to be self-reliant.

My hope for you, as you read through this book, is that you will find it relatively straightforward to wrap your mind around living out your calling, whether short term or long term, as you engage with those who will provide for you whilst you are "out there".

Part of the real adventure, we found out, is seeing just how God turns up when we have gone past our own resources, talents and competencies.

My hope for me, discovered afresh as I start to write this book, is that I will once again endeavour to apply these principles to my daily walk.

In my role as a Finance Director, husband, father, in my local church, with those I meet in my everyday life, it is possible, we can live our daily lives in such a manner that gives the God of the universe opportunities to show off, to reveal Himself, if only we allow Him room.

To be clear, I made loads of mistakes, yet God still turned up. My prayer is that you can read and remember and avoid some of the pain I put my family through. Some of the lessons however, you may just need to learn yourself, the hard way, as this wisdom tends to stick the best. But for the simple stuff, just bank it and move on!

Be blessed, find favour, and leave a legacy in the Lord.

Andrew.

Be adventurous, challenge God, challenge yourself.

Psalm 5:12. "For You, O Lord, will bless the righteous; with favour You will surround him as with a shield."

A manual for living by faith

Chapter Headings

A manual for living by faith

Missionary life, it's different

Praying for rain

Collecting Memorial Stones

A manual for living by faith

Chapter 1

Memorial Stones

It's stinking hot and raining, as only a Jamaican tropical storm can rain. The noise, as the droplets hit the zinc roof on our little church, is deafening. We can hardly hear each other talk over the roar.

We've been attending our little church, Trumpet Call, for a year now, housed in a former gym, on the beachfront at the unsightly end of the Montego Bay beaches. It's next to the local fishermen, down a track and open to the elements. One realises that fishermen are not the most middle class of residents, and I read with renewed understanding the New Testament stories and parables.

There are a couple of visitors hanging around at the end of the service. It's obvious they have no transport and they're unable to get to the street to get a taxi. They'll get soaked within seconds and will have to wade through quickly forming streams and torrents of water gushing into the storm drains. We offer to give them a lift, for which they are extremely grateful. As we pull up outside their hotel, the gentleman reaches into his pocket and pulls out some dollar bills to give to me. I refuse, we both refuse, stressing that we didn't offer a lift for reward, we only wanted to be good neighbours. He told us that he and his wife considered us to be "good soil" and it would be their pleasure to pay us a generous gift. He even went so far as to say that by sowing in good soil, they might even be considered selfish, as they knew God would reward them!

We wait for them to head into their hotel and look at the notes in our hand, $40 in the form of a couple of $20 bills. I immediately hear a whisper that this is twice as much as need, and we are to give one of the $20 bills away. We'd been on such a journey that my wife was happy to go along with this "feeling". For some context, we were currently in a season of fasting alternate days, as we didn't at that time have sufficient funds coming in to eat properly. We made sure

8

the boys never went without, but we simply ate less frequently. An extra $20 was therefore quite a big deal. So, we then drove around town with some urgency, seeing if we could spot a missionary in need of funds! We found one, another Brit, out doing some pro-bono teaching in the boy's school (Montego Bay Christian Academy) for a season. We pressed the money into his hand and told him to go and buy himself a pizza, or otherwise get blessed. It's interesting to look back on photos of that time, I look the healthiest I think I ever had. Turns out you don't need to eat every day anyway.

The very next morning, as I opened the front door to our Villa, otherwise an insect infested large shed on bricks and stilts next to a sugar cane plantation, there was an envelope on the ground. It contained $2,000 in large US bills.

The Sunday morning of the rain and tourists, we'd been in church and the offering plate had come round as usual. I literally had just $2 in my wallet, in the form of a couple of $1 bills, we were broke. I got the distinct impression that actually, God wanted it all, everything, even though it was only $2. At that moment I truly felt a strong connection to the widow that Jesus watched in the temple.

We'd recently been invited to an interview with a US based charity, to discuss the possibility of me being employed by them to head up their world-wide finance function. It would likely, initially at least, be paid, provide quality housing, in the splendour of the Virginian Mountains and would all be quite wonderful, actually. As the various projects we'd been connected to in Jamaica seemed to have run their course, our future in Montego Bay was looking like it had come to a stop. This job was a truly significant opportunity therefore. The only problem was that we'd have to get flights out to the US for the interview, and I couldn't even put food on the table every day at the moment.

The $2,000 paid for all our tickets. Our $2 offering had turned into $40, of which God had asked us to give away $20, and this had turned into $2,000. The unfolding of these events took less than twenty-four hours.

Gideon, in Judges 7:2, was told by God that he had too much. God's glory was revealed when it was obvious to everyone that Gideon was completely incapable of achieving victory through his own means and strength. God's biblical principles still work today.

Increases are routinely identified in scripture, and specifically a hundred-fold increase appears in Genesis 26:12, Mark 10:30 and Matthew 13:8 for example. In this context it's worth highlighting Luke 6:38 "Give, and it will be given back to you: good measure, pressed down, shaken together, and running over will be put into your bosom. For with the same measure that you use, it will be measured back to you."

I keep, to this day, two $1 bills in my wallet. Whenever I have occasion to fish in the back section to hunt for something, I am presented again with the knowledge that God sees, He provides, His Word is valid and holds true. It holds true today, it holds true even for me.

As I write this book, I look back particularly to our time in Jamaica. We describe the time as living ten years in the space of two. God turned up on a weekly basis, and our journals became almost nonchalant about recording the details. However, the stories of when God showed up are now limited, the memory dimming, to those where I specifically chose to connect them to types of memorial stones.

Memorial stones, today, are about your own, personal experience and using some token or thing to connect you to that specific time and place. It's your encounter with God and the physical "stone" is simply a device that brings the memory, sometimes years past, into the current.

The second fantastic purpose, as illustrated by the passage in Joshua 4, is that they are a means to share our stories with our children, of passing on the lessons we have learned to the next generation.

One evening, our eldest son Jordan screamed out in pain. We rushed to his bedside and found him clutching his foot, in which we could clearly see bite marks. He continued to scream and we realised that he'd bitten by one of the notorious "forty leggers". These are poisonous millipedes, and our Jamaican friends would say the venom could kill you. They are born with all the venom fully charged, starting off quite small, the size of a small British centipede, but could grow to be big ugly, evil looking red brutes. I'd seen one of our workers with a paralysed leg and off work for a week, after he stood on one. One of my colleagues' father, on a visit to see his son, spent a week in hospital after he too was bitten. They were grown men, my boy was small and only seven years old. I got into our car to get ready to take Jordan to a friend of ours who was a nurse. The car wouldn't start. The only time in two years a car failed to start on me and there was no ambulance to call. We prayed for help. Well, that sounds spiritual, we were properly desperate and truly felt exposed, under attack and seriously out of our depth. I recalled the statement at the end of Mark 16:18 "they will take up serpents; and if they drink anything deadly, it will by no means hurt them;" We prayed again. We claimed this scripture to be true for Jordan, right now, right here. If God is real, then His word must be real, and therefore the only logical conclusion was that this scripture was also true. Almost immediately Jordan calmed, we too calmed and felt that the danger had passed. We simply wiped an ice cube over the wound and returned him to bed and a surprisingly sound night's sleep. The puncture wound was still there in the morning, Jordan was fully fit, with nothing else to show for the night's excitement. He does however have a great story to tell.

I found a millipede encased in a clear plastic mounting, on EBay, which came from some museum tourist gift shop I imagine. That's the memorial stone for this encounter with God. The millipede still looks ugly even when safely lodged inside solid plastic. We use this toy, this memorial stone, to help recall the events of that night.

I had a distinct dream one night. I don't typically dream and remember them, but this one I did, well at least for a day. In the dream the devil came for Joel and I had to fight to protect and to save him. It was bizarre to say the least and one I woke up from in a bit of a sweat to be honest. I then got busy with the day and thought no more of it. That day and the next, we had torrential rains, to the extent that they flooded the local sewerage works. Jamaica is a sandstone island, and the water is therefore naturally filtered through the rock, without any need for treatment to make it safe to drink. The flooding had contaminated the local water table, and some of the weak and vulnerable were getting sick. Joel got truly awfully ill with dysentery. He was violently sick and projectile squirting fluids out of both ends, just the slightest drop of water and it passed right through him. I was quite scared by now. We also happened to be flying back to the UK for a visit the next day. We thought that if we got him on a plane and back to the UK, we'd be able to get immediate and expert medical care. Maybe because I'm stupid, but it took a day at least for me to recall the dream. It was like a lightbulb went off, "oh, this is what the dream was about. This is the devil's attempt to take Joel." We prayed, and claimed Joel's life back, and rebuked the devil and his schemes. He was still ill and extremely weak, and airline friends of ours said that they'd refuse to fly Joel if they thought him to be that sick.

Now, when we flew into Jamaica the first time, it was into Kingston, and then a connection through to Montego Bay. In the intervening months, they stopped the BA flights from Montego Bay to Kingston so we had a choice; dangerous four-hour taxi ride or, rent a private plane! I did some haggling and managed to blag a tiny Cessna for the same price as a taxi. Mrs M carried Joel and I carried the luggage, which we piled into the back of the tiny, tiny plane. Joel lay motionless on her lap. When we landed at Kingston, and I don't know how to this day, the plane taxied up to the entrance gate and we were escorted right through security by one of the guards, without even stopping, and right past the lengthy queues of passengers. We sat in the departure lounge and within minutes heard the call for families with young children to board first. Again, we walked right through. Mrs M just pretended that our baby boy was asleep and they let us on. The moment we sat down on the plane he started to take water without ejecting it back out again.

This episode was completely different to the insect story. I acted late, despite a warning from the Lord, and was not in control of my feelings. Joel was in danger for longer. Instead of the situation taking minutes to resolve, this time it took a couple of days or more. However, getting it wrong also proved a teachable moment! Take notice of dreams, God uses them.

We remember this particular story too. I decided to buy a joke, fake poo from a toy shop, which my boys and I still think is both effective and hilarious! As you can tell, we remember the story, and so do the boys.

We also have pictures of their stools after spending two months in India. The two months were a crazy cascade of stories and adventures, including the extreme poverty we met on our travels. Our diet and living conditions were at times fraught with the possibility of ingesting worms and other parasites. As a final check, we would take some "special medicine" upon getting to the airport to ensure that any hangers-on were expelled! The only way of checking this for certain was to physically inspect the end products.

13

That was a job for Dad. The photograph seemed like a good idea at the time, much to Mrs M's consternation.

That photo that Jordan and Joel have, their cheap fake Rolex watches, one of which worked flawlessly for many years, and their street market Kukri knives, are vivid reminders, taking them back to that special season in Asia. Memorial stones, unique to us.

You remember what you set out to remember. God is faithful; there will be times when you might be tempted to doubt that.

Joshua 4:7. "And these stones shall be for a memorial (remembrance) to the children of Israel forever."

Chapter 2

What's your vision?

People get behind a vision. Do YOU believe you are called? You need to be convinced yourself, right at the outset, in order to bring others along with you.

Those pursuing apparently good ideas, or off the cuff activities, seldom last the distance, and will often fall at the first hurdle. If you can't string together a convincing narrative for what you are doing, how do you expect friends, family and strangers to part with their hard earned cash to support you?

You need to be able to explain "it", to yourself first, and then to others. Have you heard of the "elevator pitch"? Imagine you are in a lift, or going up an escalator with someone. They ask you what you're doing, and you now have less than a minute to share with them. Do it well and you have someone at least emotionally connected to the problem you are attempting to solve, maybe a business card or even contact details to get in touch if you ever need anything. Do it poorly, nothing happens except a missed opportunity and you will feel wretched for a wasted encounter. And, maybe, all that happens is you sell the idea to yourself once again when you're tired and wondering whether it's all worth it anyway.

It's worth noting that some will back you just out of relationship. When we first started to think about raising funds to go to the Caribbean (quite a tough ask as you might imagine), our next door neighbours were the first people to set up a standing order for us. They weren't believers, and not touched by the issues we were going to help with, but they were connected to us, and wanted to support us. Trust had been built up over a number of years, and that's what they were responding to; friendship, confidence, trust.

There are many "issues" out there, and many countries where your help might be needed. In all likelihood, what you are going to help make better is already something that you are bothered by, perhaps even passionate about. What makes you angry? What sets you off? Where do you love, even though you've never been? What bizarre places on a world map are you drawn to?

I have done several YWAM training course debriefs in Malawi, these come at the end of a six-month season of classroom teaching and practical outreach. I ask the student's peers a question. "What are they passionate about, what makes them cross, where are they skilled, what countries and people groups are they constantly banging on about?" Sometimes, we are not aware of what drives us, yet usually it's evident to those who spend any time in our company. It spills out! The rest of the class always has a lot of answers, and the scribes, taking it in turns for each other, often struggle to keep up.

Please note, although most people will not "go", their passions and desires for the Kingdom are not worth any less than yours. Staying and building community, making a real difference locally and nationally is just as tough. In fact, standing up for Christ in your local community, workplace and culture can often be much harder.

I mention in the "Welcome to Leadership" chapter that some will try and place you on a pedestal as a "real" Christian Missionary, out "there" somewhere, with the Gospel. However, mission exists on your doorstep, just as it does elsewhere. Your calling is just different, and fewer people nowadays tend to consider doing it. That's all.

Never have the words, perhaps erroneously, accredited to Edmund Burke, been so true: "The only thing necessary for the triumph of evil is for good men to do nothing". A preacher once challenged those of us listening; "What have **you** done lately to stop any evil?" There is just as much evil in your town as across the other side of the world.

My vision? Hands up at this point. I do not think I did a good job of explaining our vision back in 2001. Maybe that's why we went to Jamaica with less than we needed. We didn't have health insurance, or dental cover, and we were glad to receive free housing, because we certainly couldn't afford to rent anywhere.

I'd searched long and hard for something meaningful to do, since coming to a sort of mid-life "assessment" when I was in my mid-thirties. I'd achieved my very modest career aspirations already. These basically amounted to a £50,000 salary and becoming a qualified Accountant. It was no more than a throwaway comment I made to myself when I was nineteen and starting to study for my accounting exams. In my Financial Controller role with Roche, the world-wide Pharmaceutical giant, I'd just made that salary. I had the car, the pension, the bonus and the opportunity to apply for an assignment to Switzerland to be based at their global Head Office.

I struggled with the fact that I now had another twenty of thirty years of the same thing. My corporate drive and ambition simply evaporated. There must be more to life, to work; what could I do as an Accountant that would actually make a difference?

I might add that Mrs M had always wanted to be a Missionary, and was only back in Kent after her teaching degree to finish two years of post-qualification experience. She had planned to head off to Africa somewhere as soon as she could. She then met me, fell in love and had to patiently wait whilst I caught up with her!

I explored charity jobs, mission agencies, and even VSO. I got so far as a preliminary interview with them to be told that "Accountants were in high demand, but could you just leave the family behind?" The whole point was that we would be doing this as a family, so "no". A year passed by without any movement. Then a chance encounter with a leader in a much wider network of churches suddenly opened up everything, and quickly! He challenged us simply "if God asked you to point on a map where you want to go, what would you say?" Both Mrs M and I, who had not hitherto discussed this, said the Caribbean. We looked at each other in amazement. She had spent some fifteen years supporting a Tear Fund child in the Dominican Republic. I'd always felt a random connection to Caribbean people, wherever I encountered them.

Peter, the church leader responsible for heading up their church network's overseas contacts and projects, casually said he was popping out to Jamaica in a week's time, there were a couple of projects they were connected to, and would we like to go with him?

Favour is a funny thing. We'd just got back from a week's skiing holiday; accountancy is well paid after all. So we didn't have any holiday I could book off. I'd also spent all my savings on the skiing trip. I searched and happily discovered that all my overseas trips in the past meant I had enough air miles for a free flight to Montego Bay, and that there was a flight I could take next week. My boss also, quite unexpectedly, said I could take another week off if I wanted to.

Both projects needed competent financial management, perfectly attuned to my skillset. One was a slightly out of town school, community centre and farming project. The housing would be on site, right in the middle of the site. It would be a 100% commitment, not just for me, but also for Mrs M and the boys. It just didn't fit. The other was for a Missions and Bible College. Again the housing was provided, but there was more room, some privacy, and it felt like an environment where both Mrs M and the boys would thrive. I met both leaders for interview and was now excited to take things forward. We went out a couple of months later for a family visit. It had to work for everyone or else it would be a disaster waiting to happen. It did and we flew out as a family the autumn of that year.

However, I would struggle, even now to articulate my vision at the time. It was something like; "Accountants are needed everywhere, there aren't many in the Caribbean prepared to work for nothing. Accountants are usually selfish! I can bring my skills and experience to this organisation and local community projects." It doesn't trip off the tongue easily. Whilst being valid and true, it struggled to capture people's attention. The amount of support we raised, including the church's element, was less than £1,000 per month. That had to cover everything. We stubbornly refused to wait any longer, trusting, perhaps presumptuously, that God would supply all our needs.

When we went out with YWAM several years later, we did a much better job. "YWAM welcomes families into missions. The 10-40 window, where most of the world's poorest and neediest people are, doesn't have many missionaries at all. My accounting skills would help the charities and in-country businesses to stay afloat and succeed, enabling more missionaries to go and those that do go to stay for longer." Much better, and something people got behind.

It's all about you. We've seen with the memorial stones that they help us to recall when God stepped in with us. I love water sports and listen more intently when the bible passage has water based stories. I also love Tennis and Motorcycles and listen much more intently to preachers who share these same passions. A throwaway comment from one about riding his motorcycle in Asia, lead me to stay in touch with him and spend a really valuable week in Nepal, many years later. What "catches" your attention? Listen out. I have natural skills in accounting, numeracy and languages plus I don't mind making a fool of myself. I'm happily prepared to go where I can't speak the language and attempt to get by.

Careful of experts. Careful of thinking you're an expert. Often God uses the unskilled, they tend to seek God more. Jesus in the boat (Mark 4:35) was talking to sailing experts. Jesus catching fish (John 21:6) was talking to fishing experts. Experts often don't listen, for they don't have anything to learn. It says in Isaiah 5:21 "Woe to those who are wise in their own eyes."

It's not all about you. God already has a plan, even Jesus simply watched out for what the Father was doing. Our job is to discover what God is up to already. When I was helping the training school in Malawi, we would ask them what is happening in Malawi now, and what opportunities did this present? There were Orphanages with too many children and too little support, communities with poor access to food, and villages with no access to education nearby. It doesn't get any simpler than "Love God, love others" paraphrasing Matthew 22, Mark 12, and Luke 10. We see in proverbs 3:27 that if it's in our power "to do good", then we should. In essence then, we are all called and are all equipped. It's hardly rocket science. Our western culture, and our reading of English translations, mean that when we see "you" in the bible, we immediately think of "me". My African friends see "us". That sometimes places an entirely different perspective on things. Do we keep looking for that special sense of calling, and disregard the general and always-true calling, for all of us, all of the time.

A dear friend of mine thought he had nothing to offer. He read a book describing an orphanage in Nepal. It repeatedly had to be dug out as the local sewerage and storm drains emptied themselves into their building, being located on a bend at the bottom of a hill. The writer was a poorly educated, heavy machinery operator. It struck him that all was needed was a ditch, and he'd plenty of experience digging ditches. He went out, dug the ditch, likely saving many lives and improving health outcomes for hundreds. My friend saw himself in this story and realised that God was calling him to missions.

Make sure you can do a good job of selling your vision.

John 5:19. "The Son can do nothing of himself, but what He sees the Father do; for whatever He does, the Son also does in like manner."

Chapter 3

Welcome to Leadership

You are now an expert, wherever you go. You are the real deal, an actual modern day missionary, a real Christian, living a life fully committed for God. Of course we all are, but there comes now a sort of elevation to your status, not by you of course, for surely you will be only too painfully aware of your short comings, but by others.

The first picture on page seven is when we had to pray for rain. Local farmers heard we were in town, begged us to pray for they'd not had any rain for their crops. We were the foreign Christians, and so God had to listen to us! We had no choice but to pray, and long story short, eventually after an hour or more of pressured prayer, it rained! We even prayed and then pulled in our own tiny hand-sized cloud just like Elijah in 1 Kings 18.

However, there might also be envy, some will want to know how you managed to escape the rat race. How come you get to have all the fun, when everyone else is stuck here? Wherever "here" happens to be.

You are now public, even if you simply get your church leaders to pray over you at the front of church, and even if you only get two minutes to share your story, you're now "up there." You are now being watched, and sometimes scrutiny will be hidden and it can be unfair. It doesn't matter if you want it or not. Welcome to leadership.

Money, our use of it, can be a keen indicator of our spiritual state. People will be watching you and what you do with money. This is true, and it doesn't matter if you think it unfair! Our attitude to money uncovers our discipline, whether our actions are in line with Gods heart and where we are placing our trust. Do we look to our pension plan, or to the Alpha and Omega who holds the Universe?

For a season, I spent time focusing on the book of Proverbs. This book of wise sayings was written by, at the time, perhaps the wealthiest man on the planet. It addressed many, but for me especially, three primary topics, our morals, our mouths and our money. When the Queen of Sheba sought Solomon out to see for herself, what impressed her was not only the wealth, but the wisdom, justice and righteousness of God, and even the servants.

One hears stories, and I was at one such conference by the way where this happened, of ministry/church collections where the Leader asks people to hand their wallets forwards a row and then for the other person to check the wallet or purse and decide what to give! Of course we all hear this and smile and say of course we'd be more generous if we saw a wad of notes in a wallet. But who knows if that cash had just been drawn out to pay the monthly rent or to buy medicine for a sick relative; who are we to judge another's apparent wealth?

For that season spent in proverbs, I took a pencil and in the margin, wrote a $ sign whenever it mentioned money or wealth or generosity! I suggest it would be a profitable afternoon if you did the same. What's the worst that could happen? You could have your entire worldview on money challenged that's what!

I said that as a leader you would be watched, or assessed, or judged. You may therefore be copied for the good or even the bad. Sometimes others will look to you in order to justify one specific behaviour or habit of theirs. At the first church I attended, I was pointed in the direction of the Treasurer to discuss tithing. Right off the bat, he informed me about tithing net, for what was in my pay packet and to use that as a basis. It said more about his faith than God's best for me. It taught me, for a while at least, to calculate to see what I could get away with in terms of God's (financial) requirements. It did not teach me faith, and it did not speak to me about blessing and generosity.

My question then is, "What are you modelling?" Is there anything you are doing with your money that might not be wise for others to copy? Are there any habits, little foibles of yours that you may like to consider? Unfortunately, as leaders, we are held to a higher standard than others. Oops. Mistakes and flaws get magnified. What reputation do you have, do you know? Let's make this personal to me, for ease. Do I tithe? Do I give to those that ask? Am I generous? Do I bless others? Am I always buying breakfast at a world-known coffee shop, rather than my local community café, and then complaining that I don't have enough money? Do I buy expensive clothes, and food, and shoes, and kit? Am I first or last to meetings? Do I engage in meetings? Do I sit at the back, or at the front? Do I volunteer, or hide? Am I visible or invisible? How do I speak about others? Do I stand up for others? Do I do things in secret that I wouldn't want exposed? Do I make too public the good that I do? Do I keep my promises? Am I trustworthy? Am I good company? Do I think of others before myself? A telling proverb; "what one generation allows, the next embraces".

Is there anything in your own culture that wouldn't translate in someone else's? Have you considered these things, or simply even just "enquired of the Lord"? Have you sought the wisdom of those who have arrived here ahead of you? What mistakes did they make, or witness, that you could learn from? In India and rural Malawi, women didn't expose bare legs or arms. In Jamaica, money was seen as a way of proving that God was faithful and that you were living right with him. In the UK, that's not necessarily true at all, and you would never share, or share very sparingly, with anyone how much you had been blessed! The US Church likes to ensure that their missionaries are kept well, have decent housing, good healthcare, strong pension plans. From experience, the UK church, even if unwittingly, still holds on to an old-fashioned notion that missions is hard, and that you will be poor. In the central US, and Jamaica, and

23

African cultures, alcohol is a serious issue. Just drinking could be "proof" that you are not saved even. In the UK, at the start of YWAM training courses, the leadership will point you in the direction of the best local pubs.

We had friends in Africa who noticed that local African Christians started to carry drinking bottles around with them. They'd seen that missionaries all carried water bottles and had assumed that this cultural artefact was in fact connected to being a Christian! Africans have a different tolerance and routine for drinking water, they do not need a constant-at-hand sources to keep them alive. We do. They'd seen something modelled that wouldn't have occurred to us at all.

When I play tennis, unfortunately, I have a habit of swearing and have been known to throw and even break the occasional racket. Playing tennis in a cross cultural context caused me a massive amount of stress to modify my behaviour, on court demeanour and language. I verged towards undoing any good Christian witness in several countries. I also had the privilege of meeting and playing national tennis champions in Jamaica and Sierra Leone by the way. God is good. God is creative. God knows what blesses us!

Some top tips

- Could you show your bank account to others and not worry what they saw?
  - Integrity begins with your bank account. Wise friends Jan & Mintie told supporters that their bank accounts were always open for inspection.
- Do you keep your own records of how you spend your money, if others asked?
  - They're "paying you" after all. Beyond bank accounts, there is cash and ministry and everything else. Do you know how your money gets spent?

- Are you up to date on tithes?
  - How do you know? Live it first, then you can teach with authority.
- Do you pursue offerings, or avoid them?
  - This really shows your engagement with the Lord on being generous.
- Have you thought through your culture and the one you are in?
  - Unintentional offences can easily arise. Make sure you have sought out wise counsel about where you live. Shorts for men and sleeveless tops for women may be perfectly acceptable in London, not so much in Lilongwe.
  - Maintain a clean attitude towards others - "judge not lest you be judged".
- Pray for wisdom in your finances, and how you share about it
  - Being honest does not necessarily mean giving out all the details! With your finances, have a "pot" for weekly household, or more personal expenses.

Transaction versus Transformational Leadership

I have Tom Bloomer (University of the Nations) to thank for this. I hope he forgives me for taking a well thought out, highly researched, expertly delivered seminar, and butchering it to what is effectively a sound bite! Years later, I still remember. Essentially, 1 Corinthians 10:24 "Let no one seek his own but each one the other's well-being" – Your dream or their dream, your success or their success?

Transformational leadership is when you lead a group of people, empower them to achieve their vision, to equip and champion them, to encourage them. It's about them.

Transactional leadership is when you use a group of people to achieve your ambitions, your targets. You use them, bend their will to yours, it can involve manipulation, dominance, direction. You will gladly sacrifice their best for yours. It's about you.

There's a huge difference between leading a group of volunteers, rather than managing a group of employees. Volunteers will only follow someone they feel connected to, share a vision with, and who works alongside them. You cannot simply tell them what to do, oh no. Employees however, will pretty much do what they're told, as their mortgage usually depends on it.

Consider Matthew 16:25 "whoever loses his life for My sake will find it" and the leadership style you imagine that God wants to reward, or share in heaven with the angels?! And finally, always be ready to "just say a few words". It took me a while to learn this, and a painful time that was. I am after all, an Accountant, not a Preacher. It's amazing how often you will be asked to share. Get used to it. This can range from [1] a thought for the day [2] leading devotions [3] a practical sermon on what you have learned to [4] a full blown exegetical analysis for a Sunday gathering where you find yourself the honoured guest. It happens. I sometimes struggle to be spontaneous, so I now travel with a selection of these sort of things in the back of my bible. I prepare and so am ready to be called upon. Cheating? Remember, this isn't about you. What's important is that you are able to minister to those in front of you. Remember too, your education, your bible study, what you learned at home, is often significantly more than anything available locally. You, even average you, have a wealth of teaching, education, wisdom that those in front may need to hear. In Malawi, missionary friends of ours would often pray for those suffering from headaches; they would do this and also exhort them to make sure they go home and drink plenty of water.

Make sure you have considered local customs and cultures and don't get carried away. I was invited, along with my two sons, to a Christian wedding in a remote Indian village. The only Christian family in the village was having a wedding. When I say poor, I mean that across the entire village, there were only three plastic chairs.

Everyone sat on the ground. Being the honoured guest, I was invited to sit on a chair, displacing the mother of the bride. This gave her immense honour and humbled me to say the least. Our presence, just being white and western, apparently gave this family huge honour. It would likely change their status from being persecuted Christians to being the family that were seen to be able to invite westerners to their wedding. We would later learn that this was the same area that had once seen an Australian missionary father and children burned alive in their vehicle. Despite repeated assurances that I would not be expected to speak, half way through the ceremony they called upon me to deliver a few wise words to the happy couple. I had a thought, wow, I would get to say "and now you may kiss the bride". I was excited that this would one day make for a great story. The nearer I got to this point in my address, the more I was convicted it wasn't right. Tone down my desire, keep it simple. It went well, and everyone was happy, I think. I was later told that in the local culture, the bride must display a huge reticence to leave her mother's side and be given to the man. It's a "tearing away", not a "cleaving to". I would have caused untold offence if I had suggested that an affectionate kiss with her new husband was expected. Holy Spirit, thank you. Luke 12:12 although out of context, was never more true.

Your life is now public, be aware, act accordingly.

Proverbs 10:9. "Whoever walks in integrity walks securely."

A manual for living by faith

Chapter 4

Money, Wisdom, Kingdom

Late 2007 and we'd handed in our notice to leave the Isle of Wight (Christian Youth Activity Centre) and start thinking about our journey back into overseas missions. We'd applied for a Cross-roads Discipleship Training School (DTS) at Youth with a Mission's (YWAM) centre in Colorado, USA.

DTS is the "basic training" if you will, for every one of YWAM's worldwide twenty-five thousand plus volunteers. Whatever country, whatever culture, whoever you are, whatever you do, the DTS is the common thread that binds everyone together equally. It's typically three months of classroom training, followed by two to three months of outreach, sharing the Gospel. Many simply use this as a standalone season to spend more time learning about God, taking a step back from "life", and spending time seeking what the future might hold for them. Some, a few, will use this as a springboard to move onto longer term mission work. You pay to attend and if you choose to continue on and work full time, you also pay to be a volunteer. Nobody earns a salary, nobody gets paid. All the costs of accommodation and missions outreach are borne by the local YWAM community. You need to be committed! This model is one reason why it flourishes when some established agencies are consolidating or reinventing themselves.

So, for the Meggs family, we were looking at around £10,000 for this six-month season. My boss suddenly announced that if I were to leave early then he'd make sure that my three months' notice would all be paid in one lump sum. There is a separate story of just why he wanted to move us on so quickly – buy me a coffee sometime! Wow, all our DTS and even the outreach costs, were in. I was amazed at how easy it had been to fund raise.

Except of course that he didn't have the authority to make such a promise, and I later discovered that this money would not in fact be paid, once Head Office found out about it. This was indeed disappointing, disastrous even, not least because I'd already quickly and excitedly announced to anyone who may listen (including all those that I may have asked to help us financially) that God had miraculously provided for us...

We had a choice; to trust God, honour His bride, and not bring disrepute on my boss, nor the charity, both of whom were Christian. This is where we really started to see again that God is a loving father, not in anyone's debt, and able to do anything. 1 Samuel 2:30 says "for those who honour Me I will honour". People I'd never even met asked to see us and give us money. Two separate individuals had been made redundant and offered us part of their severance payments. One was a passionate "missionary" but unable to travel overseas due to ill health, this was his way of partnering in the Gospel. Within a month, all the initial part of our training costs, including flights and visas, had come in. This time in cash, for real.

Sometimes I think this was a test to see how we would react, and whether we would trust. Other times I am convinced that God likes to show off, or at least to remind us that He doesn't need us, that we need Him!

The story of God's wisdom interacting with us looks different for each of us. Other Whitstable friends, loved missions but were unable to go themselves and would give us not insubstantial gifts from time to time. One-day God spoke to the husband in a dream, warning them to sell their investments; just ahead of the banking crisis and everything tanked. They were then able to continue to bless many other people in times of hardship.

A manual for living by faith

We will see in a later chapter that Jesus' parables mention money and the Kingdom extensively, more than being born again, salvation, sin, even forgiveness.

Seeing how you and I behave with our money can be a rather keen indicator of our spiritual state. Have we read the word of God on the subject, are we applying it, do we trust it, do I think it applies to me, today? In the bible, financial prosperity was often related to crops and livestock as it was an agricultural economy. Today, we have money as the main unit of exchange and the indicator and demonstration of our apparent wealth.

So, can we trust the wisdom of the bible? I love detail and being an Accountant I see the world through numbers.

Some four thousand or so years ago God instituted circumcision on the eight day. Just recently [McMillen's "None of these Diseases" P93) "science" has uncovered that vitamin K and prothrombin factors, used to heal the body, is at its strongest on our eighth day of life. In 1 Kings 7:23 the dimensions of the plate are consistent with the concept of pi. We may have heard of the Crimea war and Florence Nightingale "discovering" hygiene. The wisdom of hygiene had been part of the Jewish culture for so long that in 1665 Great plague of London, Jews were the only group not to be infected, leading some to accuse them of being behind it! The Leviticus washing regimes had kept them safe. Matthew Maury from the USA was laid up injured in bed, and in 1860 reading the Psalms and especially Psalm 8:8 thought that if God had mentioned pathways through the seas, then they must be there. Extensive research of Atlantic crossings, routes and times, lead us to the modern day discovery of the oceanic currents.

Yes, I believe we can trust biblical wisdom.

Jesus' first preaching words were about the Kingdom (Matthew 4:17). The Kingdom is a place where the rule of God exists. It tends to be upside down and contrary to the world's wisdom. It's about giving not getting. Centuries before, Solomon had been asked by God what he wanted, he asked for wisdom, which he received, but also became the richest man on earth. It would be good to note that Solomon made an extravagant offering to the Lord, considerably more than protocol required, at his investiture. He didn't ask for money, but a discerning mind, to be able to distinguish good from evil and acknowledged he needed help. God gave him those of course as we all know, and riches, the fame of which went around the world.

Jesus also said, in Matthew 6:21, that where our treasure is, there our heart is. You will end up giving worth (worship) to what you spend your time thinking about! We know of course that we ought to replace the word "thinking" with the word "worrying". In Matthew 6:34 Jesus explicitly tells us not to worry. In Luke 12:22 He says "Do not worry about your life, what you will eat; nor about the body, what you will put on."

Fasting is an underused resource and freely available to all believers! We'd been trying to sell our house in the UK, but were in the US. Two times we'd sold it only for house sale to fall through, the second time the purchaser had a heart attack literally as he was walking to the Solicitor's office to sign the contract! Someone suggested I fast, and I glibly said that I'd fast until something happened. A succession of people shared about three days being spiritual, then seven and then even ten. Finally, helpfully, someone said the best example of fasting in the Bible (apart from Jesus) was Daniel and he did it for twenty one days. We heard the news on day twenty one that the house had sold and someone else suggested, helpfully, maybe an extra three days to seal the deal! The house sold and we started to eat again on day twenty five. I say all this as an example of the power that lies behind fasting. We have seen friends of ours stop a fast because they couldn't handle all the answers to pray they were getting!

Now, imagine really and truly not worrying about where money is coming from. What sort of adventure would that be? After a year or so in the USA, that's where we got to, for a season. We had sold our house at the bottom of the market, and had nothing. Well I had a Casio adventure watch and two second hand tennis rackets, my most expensive possessions, plus a family car costing under a grand.

We had just about cleared the mortgage and the remaining funds were enough to buy the boys a MacBook each to manage their home-schooling. Mrs M was gracious enough to allow me to buy a cheap motorbike, knowing well my need to spend time on two wheels. With the remainder we had just the right amount to pay for a well in the village we'd visited on outreach in India. These people had lost a third of their livestock and housing during a major fire, as the nearest water source to them was a three kilometre walk away from the village. We considered this to be an eternal investment.

We were now living entirely on His resources. We searched scripture to make sure we were living right, we focused on our calling, attempting to live for Christ. Ghandi even said, "I like your Christ. I do not like your Christians. They are so unlike your Christ."

As great friends of ours (Keith & Carole) said, "We have the bank accounts of paupers yet live like Kings." We were given items of furniture to furnish our apartment, which we created out of three adjoining hotel bedrooms, and looked out up to Pike's Peak at the end of the Rocky Mountains, the sun shining bright orange every single morning. Friends gave us their cars when they went out of town. Strangers pressed money in our hands, enough to help us buy a vehicle with which to take our refugee minors, that we were by now responsible for, around and about. People do want to bless you, to partner with you, and God knows who they are. Other friends of friends knew we liked skiing and so gave us their stunning chalet in Winter Park, several times, so we could enjoy family holidays together.

32

We didn't have enough money coming in through our bank account yet we lacked for nothing, in fact we lived better than when I was earning a large salary and working as an Accountant. I could not explain it to you to this day. But, God provided, He went before us, He knew not only what we needed, but also what would bless us.

Mrs M was invited to a local ladies group which provided a real blessing of mature friendship. The Kahre family adopted us into their weekly Life group and introduced us to some amazing families, providing a sense of belonging otherwise missing. I spent long summer days on my motorbike in the playground that was the Rocky Mountains. Out of the blue, we were given $1,000 to go on holiday to New York with the boys. Our hotel was opposite Madison Square Gardens, the Hotel caught fire and the boys keenly remember Firemen running up the stairs past them breaking down doors with axes. Happy Days and long lasting memories! I even got to play competitive tennis in the local Colorado Springs league.

The less we worried about what we needed, the more God turned up with provision. I want to say again; God gave us what we needed AND what would bless us, on top.

God's Kingdom is about doing the possible and then trusting that God will do the impossible. When Jesus fed the multitudes, He only took what was there and available, using what was provided. I would rather be involved in the impossible stuff, wouldn't you? How boring to go through our lives only doing what was in our own power to achieve.

That being said, adventures are rarely much fun, and rarely comfortable when you are in the middle of them! People love stories, and the best stories are when you go beyond the usual, beyond yourself, out on the edge. Your testimony, plus the word of God, is powerful.

A challenge for you, homework if you will. Look up in the New Testament where Jesus says words like "The Kingdom of God is like." Study these passages and see if your own life is heading in that direction, or not. For example, Matthew 18:22+ which helps us understand the Kingdom principles for forgiveness.

We will look a little later at the parables of Jesus. For now, understand that money is not about what you know, rather it is about **who** you know, and we know God.

Finally, God's Kingdom is an upside down place. We've already seen that Solomon gave a generous gift to the Lord. We're told to invite the poor to banquets, to give away, to be content with little or with much. Jesus, the Lord of the Universe, came to serve not to be served. We are told to think less of ourselves. All these things run contrary to our modern world's mind-set. Dinbandhu, a ministry in India that ministers to literally the poorest and the least in Indian society, receives Ministerial level interest and support in their work. This is interest from a government that has over a billion people to be mindful of.

Indeed, we may one day find ourselves standing before Kings.

How would your life look if you lived like you truly believed what the Bible said?

Matthew 6:33 "But seek first the kingdom of God and His righteousness, and all these things shall be added to you."

Chapter 5

Money isn't everything, favour is

Favour is what you really need, not cash. In our western world, our currency is still, just, cash. In many cultures, maybe fewer than there once were, cash isn't necessarily king.

Favour trumps cash, every time; it's bigger and higher and wider and so much better.

In the US, we helped unaccompanied refugee minors from Burma. They lived with our YWAM community, and we acted as house-parents. This meant mentoring, taking them to church with us, helping them acclimatise to the west. I was asked to explain to these worldly-wise but western-innocent youngsters exactly why a bank account was a good thing. It took less than a week for her government allowance, paid into her new account, to be stolen by a new "friend" who asked for her pin. Even as an Accountant, I struggled to explain why cash was less good than having to have a bank account.

But that's not the real issue. God's favour means you don't need money. God's favour unlocks doors that would otherwise remain shut. God's favour promotes you when you aren't otherwise qualified. Just look at Daniel 17:17-21 for a moment "he found them ten times better than all the magicians and conjurors who were in his realm".

In our second year in Jamaica, my parents came to visit, spending a week with us and, to recover I expect, a week in a posh hotel. As we drove them round and up the route to the boy's school, we went past the hospital. We gleefully recounted stories about how bad things were inside, stories we'd heard first hand from our friends who had their baby delivered there. This morning Mum had collapsed in the shower knocking herself out cold. We hadn't a clue what had happened, and took her to the hospital as an emergency admission. The horror stories came home to roost, too late to comfort my worried Dad that Mum would be okay. We sat around, Mum laid out on a trolley in the corridor, through the metal detectors but no further. They have to screen for metal, as sometimes botched gang killings are followed up in hospital to make sure the job is finished. We were waiting for an hour or more, with no action, the staff saying they had other things to attend to that were more important. I recognised one of the medics; without knowing, she was a parent and her little boy went to the same kindergarten as Joel, where Mrs M had volunteered this past year. She smiled and asked what we were doing there. Mum was taken up to ward and seen to within two minutes. Favour; coincidences, things you couldn't even think to ask for. God's economy works differently.

I love exploring and adventure and to be honest it's true to say I like danger. Likely over compensating for my many years as a boring Accountant by doing ever more extreme things outside of the office! Wandering down the Montego Bay strip one morning, I stopped off for a quiet devotional on the water front. The coffee just happened to be served by a scuba instructor and after a chat about me being a local and a volunteer, he suggested teaching me to dive. I jumped at the chance, promising to read all the books during the month and then turn up for a practical session with him one Friday a month. Over a few months, and at a total cost of less than $100, I had my PADI licence. Months later and another chance encounter, and I had another friend who was happy to teach me the advanced course, again at proper mate's rates. I went on to dive with sharks, at night, through caves and coral chimneys, down to Cayman trench and all for pocket change, sometimes just the cost of the air in the tank to be re-filled. One occasion, during a season where Mrs M and I had not had enough money to eat properly, I was waved through the gates of the Round Hill Resort (once in the top ten worldwide hotels) because the concession owner "Captain" Pete's son was at a party with my youngest, Joel. Mrs M was fed fruit on silver platters on the beach and I went diving with sharks, sat in the boat alongside guests paying several hundred dollars each for the privilege. Favour. You can't necessarily buy it.

The Bible College in Jamaica had folded; after many years of poor management and debts, it had closed just a few weeks after we had moved halfway around the world to manage the operations. The events of 911 and the subsequent cessation of almost all tourist activity was the final financial nail in its monetary coffin. We'd nowhere to go, after giving all our possession away in the UK and renting out the house, so were committed to Jamaica and whatever was thrown at us. The Texas parent company was grateful that this bonkers British family had agreed to stay on and oversee an orderly closure and moth-balling process. No small undertaking, for the site spanned eleven acres, dormitory accommodation for three hundred, staff housing, guest rooms, pool, conference centre and a recording studio. There was even a chicken farm to provide meat. With the staff gone, and after we'd worked really hard to encourage all the remaining students to depart too, we were left with the bones of a former colonial estate to manage and to mothball. The 4WD Toyota Pickup, which I really loved, was offered to us, a gift. I was delighted. On another front, our car money was in the middle of a scam, being "rinsed" by some local crooks to finance their import business. We were car-less and money-less. Yet, on the way up the hill one day, I felt a strong urge from the Holy Spirit that the Toyota wasn't ours to keep, that any new owners would struggle as much as we did, and that it was intended for them. I briefly shared with the Mrs and we agreed to take the risk that this was God and He would provide anyway. We'd seen enough of His provision so far to know that even if were wrong, God is in no man's debt. I would send an email to the States and let them know that the Pick-up would be kept safe for the future owners. As I logged on, there was an incoming mail, from Texas; they'd been praying about our original contract, which mentioned providing us with meals for our initial two years. With no College, they felt compelled to calculate the value of two years' worth of lost family meals and would we be happy to accept a wire transfer of, I recall, $3,000? That money was sufficient to go to the freshly opened second-hand car place in Montego Bay and buy our very own Toyota Crown Saloon. Picture the Russian General's car in the Bond Movie Golden-Eye with blacked out windows, fridge, and all ours, for free! Favour. 2 Corinthians 9:7 God loves (*rewards?*) a cheerful giver!

That not-eating-season, by the way, was primarily because we had not done a great job in raising support (we didn't communicate our vision well). On the food front, Mrs M and I ate alternate days or alternate meals, ensuring the boys stayed fed. We'd run out of water for a week or two too, so creatively bathed in the sea most days. However, we both looked as fit and strong as ever and I don't think anyone would have noticed the restricted calorie intake!

Our church had agreed to send us out, but I don't think were entirely convinced. Quite a few eyebrows were raised at the mention of missions and Jamaica! Moving out of the college, now with new owners, meant an increase to our costs. However, due to yet another "favourable" relationship, other new friends had rented us a spare cottage on their estate for free. Favour in this case was a free home.

Favour is that Ski Chalet in Winter Park, for three successive winters. It's the free lift passes that people gave us to enjoy it. It's the cheap ski gear that someone who loved the British accent, after a fond trip he'd had to London decades past, gave us.

Just before we left the US, one of the YWAM team felt, in prayer, to give me a free flight from her air-miles allocation. Somebody sent some extra cash, out of the blue, for a debt I'd long forgotten. My beautiful wife, knowing my love for two wheels, suggested renting a Harley Davidson, as I'd just sold my motorbike to fund flights back to the UK, making a sacrifice that sometimes husbands and fathers just have to. God worked in a number of different people to bless me with something extraordinary, a few days riding down Route 1 on the west coast of the USA. The HD rental owner even upgraded my basic bike to a brand new top of the range machine with cruise control and stereo! Keith Baker had sent me a Top Gear magazine with a section called "Roads to drive before you die". If you took your picture that month to coincide with the specified route, they'd publish it. I got my picture in the next issue! (Now that's what I call a memorial stone).

Having left the USA, and our Visa application cancelled, we found ourselves, after a six-month trip through Asia, with nowhere to live, nowhere to be and not a lot to do! We'd been Trustees for a friend's charity, Mission Encouragement (MET). Catching up with Jan and Mintie one day they casually mentioned friends of theirs with YWAM in Switzerland who had mentioned some empty property. Maybe they could connect us? Two months later we found ourselves living in the Jura Mountains, a lovely cottage in a tiny Swiss village with views down to the lake and Geneva in the distance. Neighbours gave us their Wi-Fi so the boys could do their home-schooling and we were introduced to Swiss community living. Milk from the local cows was paid for on an honesty system and we were shown how to take the cream off. Heating systems, wood and a washing machine were shared by several families. We had no money, yet lived in Switzerland, among people who welcomed us like long lost family, and purpose. Favour. Who needs a house, when God has access to homes all over the planet? I agreed to allocate half my time to working in their finance office and set out to undertake a research project, looking at what I'd consider "success" in a YWAM context. Very presumptuous of me, especially when I, without invitation, later sent it off to a number of its leaders!

It was time to leave Switzerland, not least because of Mrs M's deteriorating health. Again, with nowhere to go. I prayed, and went on the internet to look for "something". I imagined that Christian holiday housing might provide a temporary solution, and happened upon "Easebourne House". I misread this as Eastbourne and assumed it was near to where we used to live. Emailing the owners, they said the house was for sale but we could stay there, for free, if we agreed to move out when they asked. Just like that, it took all of ten minutes. I later discovered my error, but it was still fairly near to East Sussex, just far away enough for us to consider our future without distraction. The house was in West Chiltington, a very expensive post code, and next to a manor house that let us use their tennis courts. Fantastic. Favour.

I received a telephone call out of the blue from Lynn. The same Lynn I'd bumped into a few years before in Colorado over a brief coffee, and one who I'd presumptuously sent the "Success" report to. He knew of a Hydro project in Sierra Leone needing competent, trustworthy financial input. Would I be interested? I found myself in Mayfair a week later, being interviewed and for the first time in five years wearing a suit. I told them I didn't want their job, but as the project matched my notion of "development" I'd spend time reviewing their accounting systems. In Monopoly terms, it was like swapping Old Kent Road for Mayfair. Favour.

We should, at this time, stop a while and think about honour and integrity, mine, and yours. Have we been honourable in all our dealings, not only with God, but also with others? Ask God to help you think through your life and assess it through these twin lenses. Are there things you ought to put right? Are there some things you simply need to repent of? Are there people you need to be reconciled to? Would those who might be in a position to bless you consider you to be "good soil"? You need to know that you are trustworthy too. God knows, He knows everything of course; but sometimes He demands that we become self-aware. Why would God bless you if you never said thank you, if you wasted His reward, disregarded His blessings, and furthermore had a pattern of doing so? As you enter into a season of deliberate and increasing reliance upon the Lord, don't keep barriers to blessing in the way! For this season, it's simply not good enough to have a clear vision that people can get behind, they need to know that you are the person to deliver it too.

Many of our own coincidences appear in hindsight to be connected to events in the past. For instance, we had let Jan & Mintie stay with us for a short season, when they were homeless, many years before. Sowing seed early, with no thought of future reward, seems to be remembered by God.

Favour is having access to things you need, things you don't even know you want. It's not just money. It's friendships that sustain you, good health that means you don't need the doctors, nor the dentist; it's connections with the good, the bad, and influential. It's people saying "yes" when they'd say "no" to others. It's a smile instead of a frown. It is travelling mercies, coincidences and fantastic stories. It's an adventure.

Money is simply one singular form of reward; favour unlocks them all.

1 Samuel 1 "Hannah asked and vowed and honoured the agreement…"

Chapter 6

What is Missions anyway?

What are you doing, why are you doing it, why is it important and can you explain it?

Do we tend to think of missionaries as being old and wise? When we recall Hudson Taylor, I imagine its' the picture of an old man with a long white beard. However, he was just twenty-one when he went off to China. Jackie Pullinger was also young, only twenty-two, and specifically told not to go!

Missions tend to be done by the young – too stupid to understand that they can't achieve their dreams for God! So they go and they do.

Jesus' final words to the disciples, and by inference to us also, are in Matthew 28:18-20 "All authority has been given to Me in heaven and on earth, go therefore and make disciples of all the nations, baptising them in the name of the Father and of the Son and of the Holy Spirit, teaching them to observe all things that I have commanded you, and lo, I am with you always, even to the end of the age."

All of us, as believers, have some understanding that this "great commission" is important and requires us to be active. Some of us will have already been part of church or para-church mission's programmes and activities. Some reading this book will be heading off into that arena, or will be out there already. Yet do we really have confidence that what we think we're doing has anything to do with what Jesus meant for us to do?

I would venture that "missions" is perhaps a much broader subject, with far wider implications, than we have hitherto realised.

There will be a wide "always true" narrative for missions, and then a "true for me" mandate to discover and implement.

A manual for living by faith

What is it?

Missions, if you had to define it yourself, might include evangelism, telling people about Jesus, good works, perhaps travel somewhere to do this. 2 Corinthians 5:18 says that we have been given "the ministry of reconciliation". Webster in 1828 defined this reconciliation as "harmony, friendship, gain, unite, win over, make compatible".

I'd therefore suggest that missions might be described as "seeing the world the way God sees it and helping to restore it to its original intent".

The Joshua Project has some amazing material, free to download, that helps us see just how far the world is away from representing God. These resources can help give you some fantastic visual aids to use in presentations and your newsletters. Terminology and maps discuss terms such as "established" (over 2% evangelical) or "formative" (less than 2% evangelical but over 5% adherents) or "unreached" (less than 5% adherents) or "unengaged" (no active church planting movement) in terms of the Gospel and Church presence. There are nearly 17,000 "people groups" (the largest group within which the Gospel can spread without encountering barriers of understanding or acceptance). Over 7,000 of these groups are "unreached". AboutMissions.org also has some great stats.

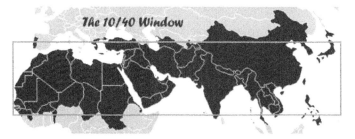

The term "10-40 window" is a Christian mission phrase that describes a land mass between 10 and 40 degrees north of the

43

equator, across Africa, the Middle East and Asia. Nearly 6,000 people groups and 3 billion people classified as "unreached" reside in this geographical area. This region is historically and biblically significant, has a preponderance of the world's poor and is dominated by the major religions of Islam, Buddhism, and Hinduism.

Mission was always God's intent. Read Ephesians 3:6-12, especially verse 9 "all people". The word "nations", or "ethnos", is mentioned some 559 times throughout the bible, in its 1,189 chapters, something like every 5th of the 31,105 verses. Each nation (ethnos) could have its own language. 1 Corinthians 14:10 says that there are many languages and each one is significant!

We have an enemy, there is a battle. The world is not in relationship with God. Furthermore, "The West" is not the world! Native English speakers number under 5% of the planet. Most missions funding and most Christian missionaries do not go to the unreached.

Why Am I doing it?

There's a great scene in the third Pirates of the Caribbean film, when Ragetti says "I'm sure there must a good reason for our suffering". Being a Christian, fulfilling the great commandment, applies equally whether we stay or whether we go. The larger question, for you as you are one of those "going", is why exactly are you doing it?

I would suggest that many of us, myself included, start with a notion that these people, whoever they are, need to hear about Jesus. They might deserve to hear, else they're going to hell, or other similar derivations. Liberal theologians might encourage us to make people happy whilst they are alive, with a great social agenda, but less emphasis on preaching, salvation, and eternity. I worked for one Christian organisation where I was asked not to preach Jesus! Fundamentalists might focus on making us happy when we die.

Essentially then, whatever end of the spectrum you might see yourself, the prevailing philosophy is the happiness of man.

When the people you are trying to minister the gospel to are rejecting you, maybe spitting at you; I suggest that convincing yourself that these people deserve salvation simply won't cut it! The wedding village we visited was in the same area that just a few years before had seen an Australian missionary and his son burned alive in their vehicle. A wishy-washy lack of conviction as to what you are doing won't work.

The end of all being is the glory of God, the deification of God, born in heaven. Doesn't Jesus deserve the reward of His sufferings? He died for them, He deserves them, and Jesus came to reconcile you to God. This motivation will sustain you much more.

How should I do it?

This is about putting your efforts into something that will make a difference. God is the strategist. He created the world out of nothing, and can create miracles for you and your ministry when there is emptiness before you. It's amazing how often we go through the motions of familiar actions, even in missions, without engaging God. 1 Samuel 10:22 "Therefore they then enquired of the Lord further."

We read stories of what Jesus did, such as in John 9:6 spitting on mud and rubbing this in the man's eyes, so familiarly that we lose the wonder, the shock, of what it must have been like to witness these events first hand! He did some truly creative things. In Jamaica I'd given up tennis but a chance encounter lead me to start playing again with a local chap, who happened to be a former Jamaican national champion, and his buddies. Simon became a follower of Jesus, partly through this season of re-introduction to the church. Playing tennis with Columbian Jimmy, which took me a while to work out exactly what that meant, was something less than ordinary. Imagine his overseas "shopping trips" and so on. Whilst I played tennis with him, Mrs M undertook a mini Alpha course with his other half, which eventually led to their baby being christened in our church, along with a car park full of white stretch limousines!

Begin with the end in mind: Ask yourself the question "what would success look like?" Rwanda was evangelised, but was it discipled? I don't have an answer for this question and am aware it raises a massive issue for many. But, it is the case that an evangelised nation tore itself apart. How many countries around the world are similar?

Reach the least reached: Most efforts go to the already reached; that's most of the money and most of the missionaries. Engage the enemy directly? God is at war with the devil, it's already an active struggle. It's not passive, we shouldn't be comfortable. Look for open gateways, where are the already-open doors? Look for key people, or strategic places. India, which is open to the Gospel, has more Mara tribe members than Burma, a closed country. The poor do not recognise borders, especially when our modern artificial countries span across nations (ethnos) and people groups. There are as many Azerbaijani people in Iran than Azerbaijan, and they can go in and out of Iran, we can't.

How do others think? (Worldview)

These are the basic assumptions, held consciously or unconsciously, about the basic make-up of the world, and how it works. Everything that is produced, even Hollywood movies, will be written through such a filter. They help us make sense of the world we live in.

Every culture, every country, maybe even every people group will have them. It will only be when you move out of your own culture will you have a mirror with which to see it. You will likely be able to see things in the new culture, coming in from outside, but be wary of challenging these until you get some wisdom!

Being British, I had a strong sense of time keeping. I would get inordinately offended in Jamaica when meetings would be late, or those in charge would receive phone calls during my meeting. It took a while to realise that actually "time" was less important here, the value was in being with someone, and time was irrelevant. My offence was over something that didn't exist in the local culture! So I took my watch off and it became, as was the local custom, more an item of jewellery.

Naturalism, which covers secularism, scientism and materialism, is defined by the lack of a spiritual or supernatural reality. Adherence (just like watching the BBC) is almost a religious fervour in itself! Large swathes of the western world see the world through these glasses. However, the west and English speaking, economically and militarily strong as it is, accounts for less than five per cent of the planet.

Then there are animism, or paganism and traditional religions. These see the world as being animated with spiritual beings. They can be personal or impersonal, often unpredictable, and must be appeased. Hinduism and some forms of Buddhism are heavily informed by this worldview.

Theism contrasts with Naturalism in that there is a God and therefore spiritual and transcendent reality. It contrasts with Animism in that there is only one God. In Theism, God exists eternally as the creator of all things. Judaism, Islam and Christianity all fall in this category.

However, the Christian God intervenes in creation and His power available to us through the Holy Spirit. Jesus conquered death and is coming back to renew creation. God is already at work, in your own

47

salvation for instance. Christianity offers hope, other religions do not.

<u>What is my role again</u>?

You have an amazing opportunity to help the church along the journey of seeing world missions, in addition to the mission opportunities on their own doorstep. There is the "always true" concept of reconciling the planet to God but furthermore the "true for you" mandate for your role within that. Most choose not to go, you have chosen to go, if only for a season.

Understand your vision and make sure you can articulate it. Understand that you are a leader. Understand that there is wisdom freely available from the King of the Universe, for you. Understand that money, although you need it, is not as important as favour.

There are over forty examples of "enquiring of the Lord" in the Bible, and punishments (consequences) for presumption (not asking)!

Acts 1:8 "You shall be witnesses to Me in Jerusalem AND in all Judea and Samaria, And to the end of the earth."

A manual for living by faith

The car

Local customs; smoking on the beach

A manual for living by faith

The widlife

Our washing machine for two months

An eternal investment

An ice cream after two months in India equals "brain freeze"!

What could possibly go wrong at this Thai Internet Café & Fish Spa?

Not the actual Malawian Hippos, same size though!

A manual for living by faith

Trying to blend in

Tourists for the day

A manual for living by faith

Another address for our post

Malawian marketing

A manual for living by faith

Sierra Leone highway, after the road washed away

Getting ready for Sunday lunch

A manual for living by faith

Water, potential electricity

Riding our motorbikes to the Nepal border

A manual for living by faith

Chapter 7

Principles (not rules) for raising funds

Most missionaries dislike fund raising, just so you know. However, given that you don't earn a salary, you'll have to do it. You may as well try to enjoy the process. Once upon a time people gave to institutions and then trusted that they would achieve their aims. Nowadays, donors want an immediate return and a better, more personal handle on their giving. Welcome to relationship with your supporters.

Principles are a great guide. Rules stifle, are inflexible, and don't always cover your situation. However, we tend to like rules; "do this and get that result". However, it can be lazy and demands very little of us emotionally. All those get-rich-quick schemes simply play on our tendency to want to get money for as little hard work as possible, they pull people in, simply because that's how mankind tends to behave!

My wife has an annoying, and brilliant, habit. Early on in our married life I'd suggest something like a holiday, or some big expenditure, and from time to time a new car or motorcycle. What I wanted was a simple "yes" or "no". What she gave me was the following; "Have you asked God, and what did He say. Whatever He said to you is fine by me." So annoying. It meant of course that I had to work, to enquire of the Lord, I had to spend time praying, and getting wisdom, and taking my role as husband, father, provider, seriously. Finally, after many years, I only go to her now with a prayed-through suggestion, one I feel I already have the Lord's approval on. She never says no in those circumstances. However, this does mean you have to get used the fact that God might say no! So, no rules on when I could get a new car or motorbike, rather a principle that I should seek the Lord first and see what He thought.

A rule might say; write this prayer-letter and get this response. A principle might suggest; relationships are what support you, invest in those first before you ask for money. A contractual mind-set might say that this or that person has money, so befriend them. Principles would say, befriend those who the world rejects and trust that God who sees all your deeds in secret will reward you! Matthew 6:1-4.

Warning, you may experience disappointment if you read the next few paragraphs.

Most churches tend to shy away from the topics of money and sex. That they happen to be the two single biggest issues most people in the entire world spend their time thinking about, is a sad reflection on the wider church, I think. We had a brilliant sermon on money recently, but in the end it got tied into a request from the church leadership for the membership to dig deep to help finance a building project. Message lost.

What this does, of course, is to leave God's teaching on money completely off the table.

In a mission or Christian service context, you are likely to be in receipt of a stack load of teaching as well as personal research into the Bible. In our own DTS for example, we had eleven full weeks of some of the best most intense and thought provoking teaching ever. As an average church goer, we get what, between twenty to forty minutes a week?

Churches tend to teach that the modern day storehouse is the church, and that all tithes should therefore be paid to the church. All well and good, except that most people don't even fully tithe, let alone have additional money for offerings that they might send your way. The Levitical storehouse was used to dispense food to the widows for example, which is akin to modern day social care; tread carefully when helping the wider church understand about giving and money and biblical financial management.

You may also find that your friends in the church, especially those that do "tithe", will take the view that they tithe and then the church decides how to spend all the money. Their responsibility in giving is dealt with. Nothing else required. Giving done. They will then tell you, sometimes glibly, that if you are called then surely the church will recognise that and support you directly. Upon wider analysis, many churches tend to spend nearly all the money that they receive internally. Just take a look at your own church annual accounts.

The practicalities!

- God is the source, not your friends, not your family, not your church.
- God often doesn't show up unless He's needed, or we allow Him, or we invite Him.
- God's Kingdom is based upon interdependence; westerners tend towards independence. So bear one another's burdens. Pray for those supporting you. It's a mutual relationship, ask them for prayer needs.
- Talk to people who are already living this lifestyle, what have they done right, what do they regret?
- Pray.
- Share your vision (scriptures, words, themes). Focus on the vision not the need. What is it that you, or the ministry you will be working with, do exactly? What difference will you make?
- Share some of the stories that make it personal and tangible. Christian Aid charity adverts on TV now focus on both a before and an after section, to show you the consumer/donor the impact that your individual gift can have.
- Get your church behind you. If you are not well known, then spend a season working for the church in some capacity, show them that you can serve and work.
- Ensure church relationships are strong enough both to be "sent" and to remain "sent". That might take time.

- Get a Life group behind you. We had one in Whitstable (mostly older ladies) who would pray for us at their weekly coffee and cake gathering. Every month one of them would write a letter or a postcard and send it to wherever we happened to be in the world. It was never about money, it was about support and we loved receiving their letters! It made such a difference to us.
- Try to arrange presentation evenings before you go, and when you get back.
- Maintain a contact list. Some people may be interested in the project, some may never be. Some may simply like you. Christians and non-Christians are different audiences, so use appropriate terminology.
- In a digital age, hand written cards and letters will carry much weight.
- Everyone you meet is a possible supporter, not necessarily a financial donor.
- Newsletters do not work if you use "hints", I know, I've tried! Direct and specific approaches do.
- Presentation is important. You are competing for about thirty seconds of attention in a busy space alongside Facebook, Snapchat, and whatever the latest thing is. (Andrew Neil suggests "YouTwitFace").
- In order of success; Face to face, Telephone, Written, Emails.
- You are a professional missionary, so act professionally. This is your job. Dress appropriately when meeting others.
- The Bible is the standard, what does it say, not what you or others "feel".
- Written "thank you notes" establish gratitude. People like giving to grateful recipients, they might even give again. Other than that it's simply good manners.
- Make it easy for people to give. Have someone at home manage the administration for you. Have a response slip on

letter requests, give addressed envelopes, provide bank details, and limit people's choices.

- You are educating the church, which is itself the Bride of Christ, so treat it like a bride with respect and love.
- Remember to highlight the volunteer lifestyle and other similar groups, both in missions where you are but also those serving locally at home. Equal value.
- What other skills do you have that you could market? This is modern day tent-making like Paul did. I started down the tennis coaching route, others may do car mechanics, or hair dressing. Could you teach English, or coach youth sports? I ensured both my sons took a TEFL course and did a stint teaching overseas.
- Make an appropriate, realistic budget. Include insurance and the personal stuff.
- Do not despise small gifts. One elderly friend of our parents gives us her egg sales, £5/month and has done so for nearly sixteen years.

Be generous!

Galatians 6:7. "Do not be deceived, God is not mocked; for whatever a man sows, that he will also reap." Matthew 7:12 "In everything, do to others what you would have them do to you." We were fortunate enough to see friends enter into missionary work some years ahead of us. Jan and Mintie (see P39) provided care and support to the many missionaries "out there" who were lonely, abandoned, and with insufficient support from their home church. Sitting as their Trustees over some years, we saw first-hand that they always acted with generosity, and yet always had enough. They prayed ahead about every individual they met, asking God what would be a real blessing to those they were visiting. The book to the church "You Fish, We Fish" was some of the fruit of their labours.

We decided at the out-set that we would be generous, modelling generosity in all we did. After all, we have a generous God, we ought to be the most generous of all people!

Ahead of moving out to Jamaica, we gave away all our furniture and almost everything that wasn't of a personal or sentimental nature. And we did it again when we went out with YWAM. We have always ended up with fully furnished homes everywhere we have travelled, and we've lived in a dozen different homes since. We gave away two motorbikes, and two cars, all of which were decent, not rubbish. We continue to be blessed with free transport, whether cars, motorbikes or cycles, everywhere we go. If you want to be receive the best, then make sure you give away the best!

<u>Water the gardens of others</u>

1 Corinthians 10:24 Let no-one seek his own, but each one the other's well-being. I once heard someone preach that we ought not to pray anything over someone else that we wouldn't wish upon ourselves. Judgement and consequence I suppose. Likewise, another preacher suggested that if you wished to see blessing in your own life, then find someone who needs that same blessing and pray for them instead. Both of these messages speak to the matter of your heart. How do you react when someone receives or experiences a great blessing? Is it joy for them, or is it really jealousy, or worse? If that's your reaction, why would the God of the universe seek you out to bless you? We wish parents and those we love at home to be taken care of, so how about finding those locally to where you are and do the same for another family.

In Jamaica, I mentioned that our car money was stolen from us. A while later and I did some voluntary management consultancy for another island charity. On the day I presented to their board of Trustees I frustratingly confided our car story to the trustee sat beside me. It turns out that he was a Bailiff (Jamaican Bailiffs carry guns) and he said he'd "put in a word" for me. We received our car money back the next week!

We learned to disassociate the gift from the giver. This enabled us to freely and liberally bless everyone we met, knowing that God's reward would come from a variety of different and completely disconnected sources!

Mechanisms change over time. Today there is Crowd Funding, Just-Giving, and of course Facebook. Eventbrite's Fundraising Trends article highlights the value of community, belonging, value and trust, personal connection and speaking the language of the donor. These are not technology dependant.

There are already some great resources available for wider and more detailed reading. Just remember that some are geared, culturally at least, to a western and USA or UK based audience.

- Crown Financial Services (www.crown.org) have some very useful wider guidance
- "Funding your Ministry whether you are gifted or not" – Scott Morton (US)
- "Friend Raising" – Betty Barnett (US)
- "Funding the family business" – published by stewardship ® (UK)
- "Wealth Riches & Money" – Craig Hill & Earl Pitts, Chapter 6 "Closing The Circle"
- "The Holy Bible" – God

Generosity is like living in a "Palace of Possibility".

Luke 6:38 "For with the same measure that you use, it will be measured back to you."

A manual for living by faith

Chapter 8

Managing Money

Stewardship is the subject of looking after what's been entrusted into your hands. This applies to you as an individual, it could also be your church, or a company, and even a country. A steward is someone who gets responsibility and authority from an owner to look after the owner's property in the owner's best interest.

Your mission, your values, your newsletter's stated interests, are all worth nothing if you do not act wisely. It's what you do that counts, not what you say you do.

So, these are some money-management-musts; you are living on money that people have sacrificially given to you in order for you to accomplish a vision you've sold them.

Live on a budget: Luke 14:28 "count the cost to see if you can finish".

- Create a realistic and appropriate budget for the work you are called to do. Research from others who are there. Cost of living varies hugely!
- Work out appropriate levels of possessions and spending. Do you need a MacBook Pro for checking emails? What is communicated to "locals" about their ability to minister, if they see it only done with video clips? Stories are better anyway.
- There are always (more, frequent) opportunities to give money away when you are in mission!
- Walk through each day mentally, and register what will cost you money.
- What is personally essential for your well-being? It could be cinema, telephone calls home, sports, or ice-cream! Many missionaries stop looking after themselves.
- Where are you serving, how will you access and pay for health-care? Dental care is often missed out and when you need it…

- What insurance is it wise to have? We ended up taking out a back-packing policy that covered us for a range of activities and scenarios, in different countries.
- How often will you be coming back? What are costs of travel to there and whilst you are out there? When is the cheapest season for travelling, it varies hugely? We flew new year's day one time.
- Research "tent making", what skills are in short supply where you are going, and can you get some training before you go? Can you supplement your income this way?
- Are you going to live in Community, where it's often cheaper, or alone, which is more expensive? What price/value do you place on privacy?

Keep good records: Ephesians 6:20 teaches us that we are ambassadors and should be above reproach. This may mean proving and displaying integrity in our financial dealings.

- What are the expectations of those supporting you? A church or larger sponsor might require written reports, or an account of what you've been doing, maybe a record of how you spent their money.
- Manage expectations! Invite limited access to a trusted few representatives.
- Make your choices ahead of time. Heat of the moment decisions are rarely wise.
- Keep ministry and personal finances separate. Make an allocation from your ministry support, an agreed value or proportion, to transfer into a personal pot.
- Keep your personal expenses separate and personal. Nobody needs to know how much you spent on bread, or chocolate, or underwear.
- Make sure that any donations given for specific purposes can be identified separately. Keep separate records of expenditure.

The technical term for this type of gift is "Restricted" income. It is given on the understanding that its use is restricted to certain or specific uses. This is a key integrity issue.

- There may however be occasions when restricted income has to be spent differently. Friends of ours in Nepal were there when an earthquake hit. Funds given for other purposes were diverted, through a deep and urgent necessity, to relief work. Make sure you communicate such changes clearly and quickly.
- Ensure that official reporting is respected.
  - In the UK, by being connected to Stewardship (a Christian Charity) you are eligible to receive Gift Aid (tax refunds on gifts received) directly from the Government. Keeping good records is your part of the deal.
  - You could also be self-employed and so may fall into income tax reporting. Maintaining proper records of income and mission (direct) expenses may be the difference between having to declare and pay tax, or not.
  - Again, in the UK, to maintain your state national insurance records, for future pension entitlement, may depend upon filing tax returns.
- You will begin to learn the true cost of being on the mission field

Your expectations will be different depending upon whether you travel for a short time, alone, part of a wider group, or even as a family. See 1 Corinthians 7:32-35

I know from personal experience that I can "comfortably" go for three weeks without eating. I managed to support Mrs M through a terribly tough two months in rural India by repeating the mantra "we can do anything for eight/seven/six weeks". She suffered diarrhoea for six weeks straight, had to wear full local dress in one hundred percent humidity with temperatures in the forties. It got to the stage where a cockroach running through her hair elicited not a response.

It was tough. I was offered refreshment at one orphanage where there were so many flies on the plate, you could literally not see the food; a case of putting your fingers through, grabbing something and hoping that by the time it was in your mouth that the flies had left! Two years in Jamaica meant getting a car, renting a home, sorting out schooling. Two weeks in Malawi doesn't.

Children need entertaining, education, bathing, they need to eat and drink safely and regularly. They need your attention; you will worry after them.

That being said, we found completely by accident, after once again going somewhere that ought to have been off limits, children can unlock favour, amongst even gangsters! One drug dealer on the beach in Jamaica became my friend, shooing the other crooks away whenever we stopped by to say hello! I was "a family man" and to be left alone. I'd simply stopped to chat to him one day with the boys.

Study Proverbs and mark a £, $ or € against every money, power or riches reference.

More wisdom: Matthew 6:33 teaches "But seek first the Kingdom of God and His righteousness, and all these things shall be added to you."

- Save, but don't hoard. You may have specific things you have to save up for. Open a separate account, or have a separate special place for things like annual flights home, your visa renewals, or sudden accident or medical bills. We had need of emergency dental care in Jamaica, with no insurance. Dental pain meant I'd have given up almost anything to make it go away!
  - Proverbs 30:25 "The ants are a people not strong, yet they prepare their food in summer."
  - James 5:3 "Your gold and silver are corroded, and their corrosion will be a witness against you and will eat your

flesh like fire. You have heaped up treasure in the last days."

- Avoid debt if you can. I believe there are times when debt can be good, such as for a house mortgage, or a business loan. Plenty of Godly people may disagree. The world we live in of course encourages debt in as many easy ways as you can imagine! However, debt makes you at the very least beholding to the lender. Debt accumulates, becomes a lifestyle and interest can be very costly over time.
  - o Proverbs 22:7 "The rich rules over the poor, and the borrower is servant to the lender."
  - o Romans 13:8 "Owe no one anything except to love one another, for he who loves another has fulfilled the law."
- Use cash, not cards; cash going out of your hands always feels costlier than the unseen, deferred pain of using a card! Studies in the UK demonstrate that people who use cash regularly spend less than those who use plastic.
- Know the condition of your flock. Okay, if you're into the detail this will read a little weird. Substitute modern day "assets, things, stuff" for the older currency of "flocks and herds". Stuff needs managing. We currently live in a wonderful old farm house on a farm, the "lawn" takes two hours to mow with a large mower! The lighter you travel, the fewer cares/worries!
  - o Proverbs 27:23-24 "Be diligent to know the state of your flocks, and attend to your herds; for riches are not forever."
- Identify your own financial goals and make a plan. "What gets measured gets done" is the well-known management phrase coined by Tom Peters. How well do you know you are doing if you don't set targets? Some example goals might include the following; and all these can be measured of course
  - o Live inside my budget, pay all my bills on time, keep up to date with tithes

68

- o Never take out a loan for a vehicle, but always use savings and cash
- o To stop work at fifty-five, then work on the mission field with my pension
- o To have emergency cash sufficient for two months
- o To give $1million away in my lifetime, or to visit fifty countries
- o Insert your own financial goals!
- Act with integrity. People notice what you do with your money. It is said that "what one generation allows, the next embraces". So too with actions you model. We were unable to play simple card games in India, thanks to missionaries who visited a century before. Do you stop regularly for costly barista coffee? Our Malawian friends started to carry water bottles, like the western "Christians".
  - o Luke16:11 "Therefore if you have not been faithful in the unrighteousness mammon, who will commit to your trust the true riches?"
- Avoid simple mistakes. Don't replace vehicles every year or two. Don't have subscriptions, they're tough to manage and control. Remove contract extras. Cancel credit cards, except perhaps for booking flights and for emergencies.
- Look after anything given or bought for you, even if its old and you don't much like it. People like to see that you look after and respect what they may have sacrificially given. You may very well need to replace that old, tired car, but...
  - o Philippians 4:11 "Not that I speak in regard to need, I have learned in whatever state I am, to be content."

YWAM have a great way of always asking "do you have the word of the lord?" It's a bit like my wife asking me if I've asked God. This can be truly liberating, what if God said "yes, why not buy a Jaguar?" I shared this thought at a church group once, but they all felt convicted, I guess they thought if they actually dared asked God, that He'd tell them stuff they didn't want to hear! But, I do believe this to be a truly liberating concept!

If you ever get asked to share, and feel lead to discuss money; suggest finding those doing things close to their hearts, locally or overseas, and if prompted to, give it there! It's the most liberating way of talking about money I've found so far! It empowers the message in a way that you asking for money would not! This is using your teaching to bless the church; after all, we know that giving begets blessing!

There always seems to be conflict when you start this journey. In the week I started this book I encountered surprising conflict at Trustee meetings, my hitherto reliable car failed the MOT, and an expected bonus from work was shelved. None of this to do with my holiness, or lack thereof, rather the conflict that exists in our world when we really start to live life for God, especially with our money.

Famous sayings: Proverbs 2:6 "All wisdom comes from God".

- The real measure of your wealth is how much you'd be worth if you lost all your money. (Anon).
- Don't tell me what you value, show me your budget, and I'll tell you what you value. (Joe Biden).
- Try to save something while your salary is small; it's impossible to save after you begin to earn more. (Jack Benny).
- I made my money the old-fashioned way. I was very nice to a wealthy relative right before he died. (Malcolm Forbes). *Sorry I couldn't resist that one!*

"A journey of a thousand miles must begin with a single step." (Lao Tzu)

Luke 12:15 "One's life does not consist in the abundance of the things he possesses."

Chapter 9

Have fun with God, play with money, and push the boundaries!

So, here's a question for you. How differently would you live if you truly and absolutely believed the bible and what it said about, for example, money and provision? How scared are you right now? Does that feeling in the pit of your stomach excite you? How liberated might you become? If you are thinking about saying "yes" to the adventure, don't worry, it is a journey, and step builds on step!

We didn't start out by giving away big things. It started of course, with a desire to see God's work accomplished and in supporting for many years a number of missionary friends. We'd started to take seriously the principle of offerings, in addition to tithes, and were no worse off, even when we upped the amount we gave away. This taught us that God is faithful, His word holds true. Both Mrs M and I had also undertaken a number of short term mission trips, into Africa and Europe, to get a taste of an alternative life, lived out amongst missionary types.

We'd also seen enough about giving away our rubbish, the stuff we don't actually need or want anymore, to know that actually it blesses nobody. In the UK, just from personal experience, we give unwanted items to charity shops, but we would tend to sell anything of real value. The real rubbish would go to the tip, but nevertheless, the stuff we give away is not, if we're honest, anything that could be construed as a blessing.

As we got to thinking about our own journey, we would be dependent upon the generosity of others so we determined to model generosity ourselves. We invited people to the house, asked them if they wanted anything and insisted they could take it away. It was quite a game, typically reserved Brits not truly able to receive with no strings attached. Soon word got around however, and some church members embraced it a little too well! We ended up with enough personal items to ship out to Jamaica, and stored things like books/winter clothes and pictures in friends' attics. It was liberating.

As you begin to see God working, it builds confidence in His word. It's not a rule, but, in general, at opportune times, "reaping" tends to happen. If you want to see big blessings coming your way, you need to be able to give big things away!

Malachi 3: 8-12. "Will a man rob God? Yet you have robbed me! But you say, "In what way have we robbed you?" In tithes and offerings. You are cursed with a curse, even you have robbed Me, even this whole nation. Bring all the tithes into the storehouse, that there might be food in My house, **and prove me now in this," says the Lord of hosts, "If I will not open for you the windows of heaven and pour out for you such blessing that there will not be room enough to receive it**. And I will rebuke the devourer for your sakes, so that he will not destroy the fruit of your ground, nor shall the vine fail to bear fruit for you in the field," says the Lord of hosts; "and all nations shall call you blessed, for you will be a delightful land," says the Lord of hosts.

Sowing and reaping. You sow seed and you reap a harvest that is based on the seed that you sow; you don't sow pea seeds and expect corn. 2 Corinthians 9:6 says "He who sows sparingly will also reap sparingly, and he who sows bountifully will also reap bountifully".

I like cars, and motorbikes, I always have. I gave away a motorbike in the UK before we went to Jamaica, and another bigger more expensive one before heading off to YWAM. I was able to buy a fantastic bike in Colorado, and was given a bike in Malaysia for the month we spent there. I was handed the keys to a bike in Switzerland the last time I was there. We gave away our Mercedes in the UK, and were repeatedly given keys to different cars in Colorado such that we never had to walk anywhere. Any trip that came up, a car appeared. Yet another car was lent to us for the time we were in Thailand.

Transport and even a driver was there for me in Sierra Leone. Sow a seed of the type you wish to receive.

Warning, make sure your heart remains clean! Towards the end of our time in Jamaica, we decided that rather than sell our much loved Toyota, we'd pass it on to other missionary friends (Art and Deb from Canada). After all, we trusted that God would supply us with a car back in the UK, so actually the sale proceeds were irrelevant. I can even now recall saying to myself "so long as we don't get some crappy old Ford Escort". A few weeks later and as we landed back in the UK, a text appeared on my phone, "good news, we've got a car for you ready for when you arrive back in the UK". Next text, "It's a 1990 Ford Escort". Oh dear. We were "grateful" for the car of course, but when we took it to a garage they said there was more value in the tyres than in the car. Laden with the family, it wouldn't go uphill or do more than fifty on the motorway. We were then given another car as a gift, wow two cars! This one we had to pay to be towed away as it was so badly maintained it was an accident waiting to happen. I think God got my attention about placing pre-conditions upon His generosity, and my heart attitude eh?

The adventure of trusting God to supply all our needs, one aspect of which happens to include money, can begin to take some truly extraordinary turns, once "in the groove" so to speak.

Jordan and I were departing Malawi after our first visit. I'd decided it would be "fun" to experience a proper African bus ride from Lilongwe to Blantyre on the way in, and bravely decided that this was too much of an experience to repeat, so we'd fly back! Arriving at the small Blantyre airport, for the short flight that would land us in Lilongwe with just enough time to catch our flight to London, it was strangely quiet. Going straight to security I asked where the plane was and got back "don't you know Air Malawi has been grounded for safety reasons, there are no flights". Hum. I said to Jordan this would be a great story one day but for now, we had less than three hours for the London flight and even if I got Daniel back again, it was a four hour drive anyway. I walked up to a couple of gentlemen on another desk, in our empty airport hall, "don't suppose you have any flights today do you?" I asked. "Why yes we do actually, one is just landing in a few minutes". I further enquired, hesitantly, about any seat availability, and there were just two! I got my credit card out to buy them, and was refused, saying only cash would work. I had no cash! However, I casually said that my good friend Daniel, a Missionary in town, would be able to bring the cash along later that afternoon, and would that be okay? He looked me up and down and then to my surprise he said "of course" and promptly hand wrote me two tickets. Later as we sat on the plane scarcely believing our good fortune, security guards entered and dragged one customer off as apparently she'd snuck on without the right ticket. Phew.

The next time we visited Malawi it was Joel's turn. Unbeknown to me, or to the Foreign & Commonwealth Office (FCO) I suspect, they'd suddenly decided that everyone had to have a Yellow Fever certificate to gain entry. [The FCO is the place to visit for all official guidance about visiting countries]. I had this inoculation and certificate from earlier African trips, Joel did not. We were sternly refused entry, not even getting off the tarmac into the immigration hall. Bizarrely, randomly, I recalled the Star Wars films when the Jedi swiped their hands saying "these aren't the droids you're looking for". I looked the man square on, waved my hand like a Jedi and said "there's no problem, we'll get it done later". He shouted back at me. Okay, I tried again, waving my hand and repeating "there's no problem, we'll just see to it later". He looked at us, and waved us through. Joel recalls that story as he knew full well what I was doing! By the way, never admit to anyone in Africa there's a problem!

Jordan and I were on the motorbike across a causeway in Malaysia, miles from anyway, had a puncture and were rescued, within minutes, by a passing mechanic. In Nepal with Mick, up in the mountains on an old Enfield, the exhaust fell off and was welded back in place for free at the next village. I nearly drowned in Sierra Leone, yet there was someone on the beach who saw what was happening and swam out to rescue me. In Burma we were followed by the secret Police, which turned out to be a fun way to spend an afternoon. Apart from me being foolhardy and taking unnecessary risks, my take on all these situations is that in living a life of trusting the God of the universe, He is entirely trustworthy enough to rescue us, even from our own stupidity.

Having given up my dream of sailing, God knew that it's something I still value. In Malawi, after a long week and my fourth trip out here with no R&R, Daniel decided it was time for some dingy sailing on Lake Malawi. All was going well until we rounded a headland and headed in to the beach, and sailed past a pod of hippo mothers with their babies! I was just far enough away, I guess, not to be a threat. However, we had to get back as evening was drawing in; we didn't want to be stuck in the bush, in the dark, on a lakeside with Hippos and Crocodiles. A lady appeared from the bush, warning us about the Hippos, suggesting we head off the beach in the other direction, and then remembered that's where all the crocodiles were! Her advice was, in the end; "I'd worry about the Hippos more than the crocodiles". It was a tense few minutes as I tried to set a flappy sail and pushed off the beach, towards the crocodiles and away from the Hippos. Life with God is not boring. Back in the UK it was apparent that I had caught bilharzia, the little snails that nest in your liver. Fortunately, Daniel suggested buying some local "medicine" just in case I needed it. Wise words, as my doctor said I didn't have it and wouldn't recommend me taking any medicine at all! The medicine worked (not an easy "cure") proving that I needed to have taken it.

A year later and somehow, after helping Mrs M's cousin with a Yacht delivery, I was invited onto the former Whitbread Challenge Yacht for one of the Rolex world race series! Stuff happens.

For this season and even now back in the UK, God's word holds true. We found repeatedly, that as we gave financial gifts away, we would be rewarded with tenfold returns. Somehow we'd switched from tithing on gifts received, to what I like to call "pre-tithing", when gifts were multiplied back to us. I recall one Sunday in church, chatting to God, I really wanted to just give a gift, and to have no expectation of reward. I was sort of testing my own heart, to make sure I wasn't getting too contractual with God. I put £20 in towards a special need, saying to God I was not wanting nor expecting anything in return. A few minutes later and someone asked if I did Consultancy work, and would £200 a day work for me if they needed me to undertake a small project for them... God was just showing me, actually, it's His rules not mine.

Try pre-tithing! See if it works for you.

If I struggle, I just take a look at the $2 in my wallet, my memorial stones, and recall Luke 18:29-30 "everyone who has left houses, will receive a hundredfold in this life".

Earlier we discussed how we communicate, making sure we don't exaggerate and always stay truthful. There are times when we hear stories that are completely amazing, yet the forensic accountant in me always has the challenge, asking if it's really true, or is it just a story that got out of hand? We'd heard, for a second time now a story of a mission's outreach into China. One of the young people who had responsibility for managing the budgets got the exchange rates wrong (by a decimal point) and so the team had run out of money after only a few days, had no access to banks and were by now down to their last loaf of bread. They gave thanks for the "meal" and cut into the loaf, whereupon they discovered that the inside was stuffed with cash! Alleluia we'd all say, and then promptly question whether the story was really true. I decided that if I ever heard such a story, I would try and discover its voracity and said this to our next door neighbours, Jeremy and Melissa. Jeremy smiled, a good friend of his from Germany was on that very same trip to China, and the story was verifiably true. Now, they later learned that it's a local custom to secretly give gifts of money away and that in all likelihood, someone in the village had snuck into the bakery to do just this. The team happened to be on the receiving end of this custom. However, the team needed money, they were grateful, they trusted God, the actual cash was significant, and they cut into the bread just as they prayed. The fact that someone had left the money meant it was no less a miracle of provision.

I am not advocating some kind of prosperity Gospel preaching here. I am simply saying that if we choose to live for God, He promises to supply our needs. Being a generous and loving Father, He tends to go above and beyond our needs, to blessing us with wants too. There are rules, principles too, that if we are generous then God is generous to us. If we give with no expectation of reward, for example by blessing the poor and those who would never be in a position to repay us, then it further appears that this appeals to God's sense of justice, and He steps in.

I've coined the phrase, "Living in the Palace of Possibilities", to describe this strange land we can simply and easily choose to exist in. The upside down nature of Kingdom living allows God to intervene in so many ways, and money is just one of them. It's truly exciting, I dare you. You will be able to dine out on the stories for years to come.

You cannot out give God. Generosity is itself a journey.

Luke 6:38. "**Give, and it will be given to you: good measure, pressed down, shaken together, and running over will be put into your bosom. For with the same measure that you use, it will be measured back to you.**"

A manual for living by faith

Chapter 10

Communications & Communicating

In talking about money, the assumption is that you need it. You may have a small temporary need, or indeed a large and long term requirement. However, if you are one of the few that are self-funding your ministry, might I suggest that taking others along for the ride will ultimately make it more meaningful?

You will need to communicate your story, and your needs; to different people, in different ways, at different times and in different places, across different seasons. Get it right and you have a community alongside you, even if you are physically alone, you can be part of helping the wider church to get involved and share the privilege of service. Get it wrong? Less funding, less engagement, and ultimately less fun.

Whenever and wherever and however you communicate, you will be imparting not only the message you intend, but also quite likely something of your personality too.

This area covers fund raising before you set out, asking others to partner alongside you in prayer, their moral support, being your advocate at home, and yes money. You will then need to sustain yourself whilst away. The longer you go for, the more structured and deliberate you need to be. Once back home again, whether for a visit, a rest or even for good, there will once again be the opportunity to engage people with your vision, and finally to bring an orderly closure to the venture.

It's important and sometimes a little fraught with danger.

Communication possibilities;

- In person to friends and family
- Within church life groups

- At church, to elders/ministers and maybe to the wider church itself
- As you get asked to give a talk, or say a few words, especially if you are connected to a well-known international charity
- With a carefully crafted newsletter
- Through funding request letters or newsletters
- On Facebook (other platforms available)
- On a blog or even a website
- To every person you meet, wherever you happen to be, whatever you are doing.

So called "donor ministry" to coin a phrase we heard in the US, is a part of your calling. You do need to communicate to your supporting base what you are doing, where the vision is going, your successes and maybe even failures. On the money front, common sense practical sales and marketing theory teach us that it's substantially easier (10x) to keep existing donors than to replace them with new ones. Dedicate yourself to your Donors!

This donor ministry takes time. When we were working with YWAM ourselves, it was suggested setting aside an entire morning, afternoon or evening each week.

- It takes time, effort and is best done with a plan.
- "Segment" the list, as different groups exist! You will share stuff with your family you wouldn't necessarily share with the church missions board
  - After a season of danger, confusion and sudden change, I happily shared the good news that I'd been able to learn scuba diving, in a newsletter. That came back a few different ways, one of which was to suggest that some donors weren't aware "they were paying for me to be on holiday..."

- Appreciate your donors, you are in relationship with them, if not at least in partnership, why not send them birthday cards, or Christmas greetings.
- We once took ten rupee notes from India, laminated them to make book marks, and had Christmas gifts to bless donors, at the same time reminding them of us!

You communicate verbally and non-verbally

- Your dress code when you go for meetings (did you ask?).
- How well turned out are you, do you represent **them** well?
- You can always dress smart and make it casual, not the other way around.

1st Impressions, always, still, count

- Newsletter, email, telephone call, in-person meeting, presentation.
- You never get a second chance to make a first impression.

Consider how you make your presentations

- If you use PowerPoint in Malawi, will they believe they cannot unless they also have similar technology?
- If you have the latest IPhone in a country still using Nokia's will they ever get to see past the messenger's apparent (relative) wealth?

Notes

- Make sure you get the facts straight, this includes references and links.
- Always be prepared to share, about you or the ministry. Have these in the back of your bible, or in your wallet, it's amazing how often you will be asked!
  - Short personal testimony
  - Five-minute thought for the day

- o Your latest exposition
- Don't exaggerate, your personal testimony and encounter stories are amazing enough without bumping the adjectives up and distorting the truth.

Love your audience

- Mark 12:31 "Love your neighbour as yourself".
- This is about God's Kingdom, it's not about you.
- Doesn't matter if it's a large gathering or a small group.
- Often you will be part of God's plan to help mobilise the local church into action.
- What does the church need? Have you asked the Pastor what he would like?
- Pray and ask God is there anything specific and relevant to the local church He wants you to deliver?

Use appropriate examples

- I had a "fantastic" testimony about Windsurfing and Ephesians 3:30. Except in the context of rural India of course, they had never even seen the sea, let alone a Windsurf board, so simply stared politely but blankly, as I blundered on.
- I happened upon the Cadbury story in chapter twelve, and of course they all knew Cadbury's chocolates as a recognisable brand in every Indian corner shop. That story worked really well, but of course it was only accidentally appropriate.

Establish your credibility early on

- Who are you to be standing there, writing this missive, sending this report?
- Especially if **you** are new on the scene, then use the history and accomplishments of your organisation to display your credibility.

- If you are a qualified something in the west, use that professional standing to add gravitas. I am a qualified Accountant for example. Professional qualifications always go down well.

Learn from people who do it well

- What do they do? What lessons have they learned?
- How do they approach living by faith? Have they been doing this long?

Learn from those who have failed

- Those leaving the mission field, buy them lunch and listen to their story.
- Bless them, they're probably tired, traumatised and need some love! At least buy them a coffee, ice-cream or lunch.

What works for you? You are an individual with tendencies and preferences;

- DISC profiles help you understand your own communication style and preferences; details, stories, relational, detailed.
- But crucially, it can help you to recognise how others may prefer to receive that same information.
- You can then tailor the story to the blessing of the recipient. This is loving your neighbour! If they only want the facts, telling them some long-winded story may be the opposite of what motivates them!

We were fortunate to work alongside some extraordinary people, when in Jamaica and with YWAM. We lived and worked in the USA and Switzerland, undertook substantial trips across Asia (India, Thailand, Malaysia, and Australia) and later on into Africa (Malawi). With my own consulting company, I was also privileged to spend time in Sierra Leone, Cameroon and Nepal. Into each country I brought my own cultural baggage and my personality driven communication style. Within each country were the same types of preferences amongst those people meeting me. We then too had supporters and interested parties who themselves were in and from completely different countries.

"3D Communications – Getting your message right in a globalised world!"

Tamara Neely, from YWAM, shared some great insights under this banner. I hope I do her piece justice in attempting to reduce it down to a few meaningful paragraphs.

Years ago, a "missionary" would have produced a newsletter which would have likely been displayed at the back of church, or stuck on the fridges of family and friends. Nowadays, increasingly so all over the world, YWAM itself (or whatever group you are affiliated with) will have an online reputation. Likely too that only the negative will rise to the surface. Your own communications are likewise populating a range of the following; Facebook, Messenger, Snapchat, YouTube, blogs, websites, Twitter, LinkedIn, WeChat and others appearing all the time. These are available at all times, to anyone with the skills to look them up, likely forever. This wider group could include critics, Pastors, Parents, Government Officials, next door, and the people group you are evangelising to. When we visited in India, amongst people who had never ever seen a white western child, they all had smart phones.

3D communication is a challenge to speak and live a unified message that makes sense to this whole audience;

1. The people we want to present the gospel message to,
2. The Christian audience we wish to support and be involved with us,
3. The secular, other-faith or governmental audience who might be reading.

Other government agencies, and in all likelihood with recent revelations even our own, do read what we post online!

Friends of ours described one trip where a young eager short term participant had produced a newsletter detailing how he was going to bring salvation to country X. He was rather dismayed to be stopped upon entry by officials who asked him what he was doing there, then challenged him when he shared something about being a tourist, by producing his newsletter. He was put back on the next plane home.

The 3D Communication teaching itself is more detailed and thorough, but still easily digestible in an afternoon. I encourage you to spend some time with it. It asks questions of your motivation, integrity, wisdom, and boldness. Your communication skills and outputs will be improved.

For now, though, sufficient is the question; can you share your newsletter or FB post with those sending you, the people you are going to and have it read by those interested bystanders?

Perception is indeed reality. What is written is almost irrelevant, insofar as how it is received. Be mindful of unintended communication.

John 18:20 "I spoke openly to the world…and in secret I have said nothing."

Chapter 11

How do you want to be remembered?

One of the concepts that the YWAM base in Colorado encouraged, was to "begin with the end in mind". To ask the question "what would success look like"? This is a crucial way to understand that long term, whatever work gets planted, it's only a success if it can run after you've left. It helps you stay on "on task" with your mission.

I've adapted this concept to apply it to missionaries, especially when they consider their time on outreach but also when they eventually return home, wherever and whenever that may be. What are the stories that they would wish written about them, by the people they've visited, amongst the group they worked alongside, and those sending and supporting them? The idea is to consider their actions, their communications, the impression, and the legacy they want to leave behind. It can be sobering and challenging. It forces us to consider the way we are, what message we communicate, and it stops us from being self-centred or adopting a "poor me" attitude.

George Cadbury lived 1839-1922, and created the Cadbury Chocolate Empire with his brother. They loved cricket, football, golf, hockey, tennis and God. As their factory grew, they wanted it to reflect the teaching of the Bible, for they were Quakers. They built houses, and gardens, paid generous wages, they built community swimming pools and cricket pitches. 19th century Britain typically had a 15-hour work day. Cadbury introduced (pioneered) half day Saturday and Bank Holiday closing. They set up playgrounds for children, and gave their workers free medical and dental care. On occasion they would close the factory for the staff to play cricket and one day played with a new-fangled device called a "bone shaker". It would be the modern day equivalent of buying a "Segway". They gave this to the staff member who could ride it the best. When George Cadbury died, some sixteen thousand people turned out for his funeral.

Gordon Bennett 1841-1918 was the son of the founder of the New York Herald; he sponsored a travel correspondent, famously the same Henry Morton Stanley who found the "lost" "Dr Livingstone I presume" on the shores of Lake Tanganyika. He sponsored a racing yacht, flying races and motor sport. If the stories are true, he once bought a restaurant to gain a window seat and left the title deeds as a tip to the waiter, and would burn dollar bills in his fireplace to keep warm. For many years, especially in the UK, and I remember my father's generation using it, the name "Gordon Bennett" was a swear word, an expletive.

William Booth 1829-1912 was a British Methodist preacher who founded the Salvation Army. This organisation has now spread from London to become established all over the world. Their work was one of salvation, but alongside this they brought practical help to the poor and destitute. At that time, in the 1860s, the poor were persecuted and cheap alcohol a scourge on the streets of London. Salvation Army members, many of whom were women and many also under the age of fifteen, were injured in protest marches and some would die for the cause. It might be hard to consider that less than one hundred and fifty years ago, the age of consent was just thirteen. They helped change that. In his later years, opinion eventually changed to one of favour and he was received in audience by kings, emperors and presidents. Thousands turned out for his funeral.

Hetty Green 1835-1916 inherited a large fortune from her father, maybe around $7million, and shrewdly invested it to grow it to around $150million (some $4billion today) at her death. She was described as the world's greatest miser. She is reported to have dressed her own son as a pauper to get free medical care for an injured leg; he was found out and subsequently turned away. Later, the leg had to be amputated due to the delay in obtaining treatment. Apparently she had an argument with a maid over some milk and died of a heart attack brought on from apoplexy! She is called, or remembered as, the Witch of Wall Street.

You and I may never have the world renown that the above four characters did. However, we have family, friends, acquaintances, supporters, work colleagues, sports club team members and children. In today's world we are free to travel and interact with people from all over the globe. You will have an impact, people will know you, they may know of you.

How do **you** wish to be remembered?

Whatever the answer to that question may be, the journey to making it a reality starts today, it starts now, it includes; what you say about others, what you spend your money on, how much you smile, how often you complain, what you complain about, what you get angry about, what causes are you passionate about, how do you spend your leisure time, who do you hang around with, what's your language like, do you model Jesus, are you fair, are you generous, do you volunteer easily, do you allow others to shine, do you ask questions of others, do you consider them to be of value, is it more important to hear their story or to share yours?

It can be quite a long list. I suggest that you are not able to attend to all the above using the power of self-belief and your own efforts! This sort of task requires you to be in relationship with Jesus, and to have the work of the Holy Spirit in your heart and mind.

When we were in Colorado, the newly appointed senior Pastor at New Life church shared with us that the only group really helping the poor and destitute on the street of Colorado Springs were the Salvation Army and they had run out of money. That Christmas the usual special offering was taken up and given entirely to them. Their reputation has continued and the work continues to this day. William Booths legacy is integrity. Next Christmas, during a season where the church's huge mortgage was under threat, the Pastor used the offering to clear the mortgage of another local downtown church. New Life, to my knowledge, despite all the challenges, didn't miss a mortgage payment. Sow a seed of the type you want comes back to mind.

How about some of these, very ordinary folk, who ended up doing extraordinary things?

Malala Yousafzai – youngest ever Nobel Prize winner. She blogged about school for the BBC, aged 11, when the Taliban banned female education. She survived an assassination attempt and now campaigns for rights to education.

Amelia Earhart – adventurous aviation pioneer and the first woman to fly solo across the Atlantic, who disappeared in 1927 whilst attempting to fly solo around the world.

Rosa Parks – who stood up for her rights by remaining seated on a bus and whose simple action sparked a long-overdue movement for equal rights for African Americans.

Dalai Lama - Buddhist spiritual leader, Nobel Peace Prize-winner who campaigns for an independent Tibet.

Lisa Ling – journalist, who travels around the world delivering coverage on controversial international and domestic issues.

Ann Frank – famous for hiding from the Nazis in Holland, but also for forgiving those who committed atrocities. The family friend who helped, Miep Gies.

Florence Nightingale – who eased the suffering of soldiers in the Crimean war. The Lady of the Lamp's nursing techniques laid the foundations for modern nursing care.

Emmeline Pankhurst – political activist who helped women, and men, gain the right to vote in 1918.

Nelson Mandela – first president of the free South Africa, freedom fighter turner world renowned and favoured leader, who managed to dismantle the legacy of apartheid and a world-wide inspiration.

Mahatma Ghandi – leader of nationalist movement in British-ruled India who employed non-violent protest for independence and inspired movements around the world.

William Wilberforce – politician, philanthropist and leader of the movement which would one day abolish the slave trade.

Aki Ra – as a boy the Cambodian Khmer Rouge chose him to be a child soldier and lay thousands of land mines. He then started, on his own, to clear the mines he had laid with nothing but a knife and a stick. He later set up an NGO and adopted victims of the mines.

Margaret Thatcher – first female British Prime Minister, nicknamed the Iron Lady, whose legacy still divides opinion most strongly. The Economist said "she changed the world".

Daniel Barenboim – pianist, conductor, Reith lecturer who unites Palestinian and Israeli musicians.

There will be examples in all our cultures, and ones deserving mention more than these. Many will have started off doing ordinary things and then deciding that they would not allow obstacles or injustice or money to stop achieving their dream. Just like you.

I use a Cadbury's chocolate bar as a visual aid, a memorial stone, to help students recognise the importance of their legacy and ask them to consider how they behave, now. Set the course young and early.

At home - you can be the peace-maker, who doesn't shout or raise their voice. The one who calls Mum or Dad regularly, regardless of whether they were great parents, who tells their children that they love them and are proud of them, reads to younger children and watches others play sports. You can be the one to bring flowers, the first to apologise, and looks for ways to bless those around you.

89

At work – you can be on time, one who doesn't clock-watch, who makes the tea, sometimes brings in biscuits, remembers birthdays, and volunteers when there's that emergency that needs extra help. You can be the one who does not speak about the boss behind their back, yet manages to remain loyal to everyone else.

At Church – you can be the one who supports the leadership, and if disagrees finds an appropriate time or method to ask the question, the one who helps others, who sits and listens to the stranger.

In your local sports club – the one who doesn't swear (note to self) who praises others, and who congratulates the winner with no sense of resentment and who includes the less able or less talented.

With your money – you can tithe, but you could also be the one who blesses others without them knowing who it was (like my wife), you can buy the coffees with a smile because it's God's money anyway. The job and education and opportunities you have, are largely an accident of birth place anyway aren't they?

With your time – you can volunteer, use your holiday to visit abroad, or spend time in community projects, and even learn a language. You could take a season out and commit a year, or more, to an overseas project that will have an impact on generations of people.

These things are easy and entirely within your gift today. Do them and you will already be on the journey to being remembered well. Continue doing them and with the Holy Spirit's leading, who knows, one day you may end up on the list. Yet, regardless, you are already in the book of Philippians 4:3.

Begin with the end in mind – set the course now.

John 14:12-13 "Most assuredly, I say to you, he who believes in Me, the works that I do he will do also; and greater works than these he will do, because I go to my Father. And whatever you ask in My name, that I will do, that the Father may be glorified in the Son."

Chapter 12

Coming back - The Debrief

If you are a missionary, or whatever term you will be using, you will probably have to go somewhere, whether elsewhere in your own country, or overseas. At some time then, you will be coming back, for a rest, all done in after an extended season, back for good, or to recover, train and then head back off again.

On the road out of the Port of Dover, which is the main sea-route from continental Europe into the UK, there is a sign; "Drive on the left". I always used to think this was for our European neighbours, to instruct them that we drive on the left over here, not on the right. And just in case you think it's us crazy obstinate Brits being stubbornly different; Japan, Australia, most of the Caribbean, Cyprus, India, Ireland, Hong Kong, Thailand, Singapore, South Africa, New Zealand, Malaysia, Malta, Kenya, India and others all drive on the right. My Policeman father explained to me however, that this sign is actually put there for returning Brits. Apparently we all actively consider and set our brains to the new venture, we reset our thinking to driving on the right as we depart the car ferry in Calais, France and those entering the UK calibrate their driving to the left. What happens when we return home again, is that because it is familiar, we don't even think about re-aligning our road positioning. Most of the accidents are Brits crashing because their brains are still in France!

And so it is for us when we return "home" after a season in missions. It can be after a couple of years in Jamaica, as it was for us, or after just six months on a DTS in Malawi.

Most Mission organisations, voluntary organisations such as VSO and some churches will have a "Debrief Policy". This is a set of guidance for all returning participants, and is designed to help them make sense of what they've done, where they've been, what they've seen, what was good and what was traumatic. Good debrief will also allow them, encourage them, to think about how to process all of this in relation to what they will be doing next.

Upon our return from Jamaica there wasn't much of a debrief process. Being the first missionaries our little church had sent out, they were learning as much as we were. I genuinely thought that everyone would love to hear all about our experiences, our highs and lows, and what spiritual insights we'd acquired along the way. However, most people were not that interested actually. Their own lives were still as busy and as full as ever. Much as ours were of course, before we jacked it all in for missions. Try as they might, there were not too many who could suddenly create space enough for us to share honestly. It hurt, being honest. We thought they'd be more interested. We had so much to share, so many stories to tell, so much wisdom to impart... When we eventually returned to the UK, ostensibly to consider our next mission steps, it was a case of metaphorical pats on the head, "welcome back to the real world", and get back in step with everyone else and stop mucking about.

A couple of church leaders in our current church spent two years in rural Africa, and it was a distinct challenge. Unfortunately, there was not much de-brief support for them when they came back. I could see the pain rearing its head from time to time.

So, I would encourage you, exhort even, to request a proper de-brief. If your church, or agency, is unable to supply expert provision in this area, then there are mission agencies whose job it is to do so. Find them, and use them, I would go so far as to say you ought to pay for it yourself, if your church/agency will not. It's worth that much.

Find true friends who will allow you appropriate time to share some of the best and the worst experiences. This might mean a visit to the pub, or a coffee shop. It might mean long walks. There will be a few who will surprise you, those you didn't know that well who suddenly do take an interest. Treasure them. You don't need quantity; you do need quality.

I used to describe this process like fishing; you cast your line and bait out, knowing that most of the fish won't bite, but, every now and again you'll hook a fish. Listeners will be much like this, you can throw a line out such as "oh I saw something like that when I was in Thailand" and see if anyone responds. Most won't and actually, honestly, that's okay. The few who do will provide all the listening and counselling you need.

Hopefully you will have kept a journal whilst doing this thing, whatever it was. Mrs M writes copious journal entries, all of which help her make sense of what's happening in the "now". I tend to write highlights and then struggle to recall what my cryptic notes meant when I look at them, sometimes only months later!

If you travelled with family, or a group, stay in touch. Why not meet up in a few months' time. There's nothing like a shared experience of hardship to help you bring you back again. Hopefully there will have been a group debrief before you left "there".

You will have most likely changed in the time away. Those at home, will have moved on themselves too, and may have filled in the gaps in their lives that you used to fill. Such friendships may prove to need a transition all of their own, some stay changed always. Recognise this return as God's will for your life, and this is His way of leading you into what's next.

Anything unresolved from home, before you left, will in all likelihood still be there waiting for you. Is there anything left unresolved from your time away? Reflect upon what you learned, and what you have seen. Ask yourself what the Lord did in you during this season? Are there any obstacles that might hinder you from applying these new values and insights into your life?

To help you work through your own debrief, I offer the following;

- Find creative ways of remembering some of the stories and events you have experienced. This is why I started with memorial stones. In years to come, you'll remember well these stories, others will fade.
- Write down the reasons why you undertook this project, whether that be a three-week church mission trip, a six month DTS, or even two years away with Mercy Ships. Did you have a personal vision for or expectation of this season?
- Can you summarise the precise calling and vision of the organisation you went to work with? What did they do, what do they accomplish, and what difference do they make?
- If you received training and had lots of seminars, such as eleven or twelve weeks of classroom topics in YWAM DTS; write up a highlight sentence or two from each speaker and their topic. Think about the two or three things you feel you would most want to recall in say ten years' time, when you look back again.
- What did you learn about yourself in this season? I confirmed my dislike of community living! But I also discovered I could comfortably stand up in front of large groups of people and deliver teaching, providing I had prepared.
- If there are unresolved or fractured relationships, how will you attempt to resolve them?
- Can you identify any areas where your attitudes have been changed? This might be in relation to your home country, the other country, or other cultures, and even your own future?
- Are you able to explain these changes to family and friends?
- Was there a ministry that really touched your heart?
- Do you now feel called to a special country or cause?
- In the light of the experience of this event, what are some of the ways you want to change and what will do to make these changes a reality?

- You have likely made a significant investment in this whole experience, or someone else who paid for it all did at least! This is a chance to consider it all.
- Could you write yourself a letter, with the above reflections?
- Determine to "finish well". This season may well have been the most challenging and difficult period of your entire life to date. There might be things unresolved or weaknesses surfaced. It may take a determined stand from your innermost being to say to yourself that you will wrap this all up well.
- Maintain your relationship with God, keep a learning posture, show the fruit of the Holy Spirit, and leave a positive legacy.
- How will you maintain links with the outreach location, mission partner, or country if you are returning back home?
- Do you have an idea of where you see yourself in two years' time, five years?
- Do you have a special scripture that summarises this time?

When leading a DTS debrief teaching, to help them make practical sense of their experiences, I get the participants to prepare a written statement. In ours and other friend's experience, sometimes all you get when you return home is a three-minute slot at the front of church. That's likely your main opportunity to encapsulate (in YWAM DTS for example) six months of teaching and practical experiences.

So, they are required to write this document and then practice delivering it in front of their peers. It covers some of the elements that they will have worked through in this chapter. They have to try and summarise all of that, all of their experiences, into a single three minute stand up presentation. It's tough, but it does prepare them for going home. They do this whilst "there" and it gets them thinking about driving back on the left again.

It's the chance to imagine your experience to a wide audience, like casting bread out onto the waters. I always suggest thinking of a story that is at your expense, this will usually get the congregation laughing and on your side sympathetically, especially if it's some kind of cultural faux pas! You'll have just enough time to explain what the organisation does, where you went and a summary of what you did. Explain what you got out of it, and any difference your trip was able to accomplish. It's the time to thank the church, and supporters, both for prayer and finances, that enabled you to go and do this and to recognise that it was indeed a privilege that most do not get to do.

This presentation is worth your investment, it will keep doors open, prompt interest in certain individuals, and is a neat way of wrapping up your season by "finishing well". It's important too for the church, as it neatly concludes their investment in a short term project. You can use this to lay the foundation for your future plans too if you have them.

So finally, can you combine being back home, working, and still being connected to "missions"?

Yes. Self-funding missions can be an easy way to stay connected and many do this. I myself only work a four-day week as Finance Director so I'm available for Kingdom projects 20% of my time. I ran the finances for a Middle East Refugee Agency for example on a part time basis. However, one advantage of receiving support is that you are in relationship with your donors, and this keeps you accountable. More than that, it helps everyone else, unable to go to the field, to take part in mission. Hudson Taylor's praying ladies and the Whitstable ladies group for example. Allow opportunities therefore for others to be included in the grand adventure, your adventure, the Great Commission, missions.

Coming back is just as hard as going away.

Mark 5:18-19 "Go home to your family and friends. Tell them about the things the Lord did for you. Tell them that the Lord was good to you."

A manual for living by faith

Chapter 13

And finally, currently, today – are your stories "fresh"?

My final piece of advice is not to live for too long on the old stories.

The older I get, the quicker time passes by; memories and events, often still fresh in my mind's eye, took place increasingly long ago! It becomes easy to live off old stories and yet they become ever less relevant to those who hear them. You'll know yourselves the difference between something that happened to your friend last week, compared to a story from a decade past.

We know that God's mercies are new every morning (Lamentations 3:23). We also know that God required the Israelites to depend upon Him each day, and therefore the manna in the desert was only available one day at a time (Exodus 16:21). And so too, our stories and testimonies and examples of God's faithfulness to us, should be. I certainly think they are better if more recent.

Being invited one time to address a DTS in Malawi, I prayed and asked the Lord for a fresh "now" testimony. Oh dear. Of course, one asks God for an answer to prayer, He provides; but testimonies rarely come without a "test". I'd quite forgotten that the adventure of trusting God is seemingly accompanied by some kind of disaster that He rescues me from!

Just before the trip to Malawi, I was made redundant. At other times, cars broke down, contracts were lost, and unexpected bills arrived.

However, staying true to my own advice as I write this, I do have two current events that are indeed "now" stories. The older and better connected one gets, the easier it is to make up travel plans and go with good ideas, not always God's best of course. My desire is that God would bring the opportunities He wants me to attend to. So, I prayed just recently to ask God whether there was a mission's event, some need, a trip that needed doing this summer. I have the freedom, now I work part-time, but currently a lack of resources.

Three days later an email arrived, asking if I could attend and speak at a "Business as Missions" training event in the US on the subject of Accounting and Missions, with all my travel expenses paid. That's three days for the answer to a very specific prayer.

I write down specific words I feel God is saying and keep these in small moleskin journals. Just this past week we have, unexpectedly, been given notice to vacate our long term rental home by July 31st (2018). This could be worrying, as I don't have great credit to find a new rental; long term missions and two redundancies don't help.

But, as I was praying today, I was reminded of words given to me some years back. They were about entering into a seven-year season, leaving Switzerland to work in the UK, to establish a home and help my sons through University. The day we left Switzerland for that seven-year season was July 31st (2011). God is and was, and has always been.

Make sure you ask God to keep your stories and testimonies fresh and "now". Be warned though, stuff happens if you do!

Psalm 115:12 "The Lord has been mindful of us; He will bless us."

Printed in Great Britain
by Amazon

18568696R00058